LOS ANGELES:
The Enormous Village

"When I came here to live in the early 1920s, I found what my friend Louis Adamic so aptly described as the 'enormous village.' Even then it was not yet a city. But in a matter of two decades or so Los Angeles became—well, Los Angeles."

—CAREY McWILLIAMS

Courtesy Security Pacific Bank

Angels Flight
(1901-1969)

Los Angeles:
The Enormous Village
1781 - 1981

JOHN D. WEAVER

CAPRA PRESS
Santa Barbara
1980

BOOKS BY JOHN D. WEAVER

Fiction
Wind Before Rain
Another Such Victory

Non-Fiction
As I Live and Breathe
The Great Experiment
Warren: The Man, The Court, The Era
The Brownsville Raid
Los Angeles: The Enormous Village

Juvenile
Tad Lincoln: Mischief-Maker in the White House

Copyright © 1980 by John D. Weaver.
All rights reserved.
Printed in the United States of America.
Some of this material has appeared in a slightly different form in *Travel & Leisure* and *Westways*.

Cover photograph courtesy of
the *Los Angeles Times*.
Other photographs edited by
Robert A. Weinstein.

Library of Congress Cataloging in Publication Data

Weaver, John Downing, 1912-
Los Angeles: the enormous village.

Includes index.
1. Los Angeles—History. I. Title.
F869.L857W4   979.4'94   80-17366
ISBN O-88496-158-3
ISBN9-88496-153-2 (pbk.)

CAPRA PRESS
Post Office Box 2068
Santa Barbara, California 93120

For Harriett

Who crossed the plains in a covered Chevrolet to homestead in the Hollywood Hills, (circa 1940)

CONTENTS

I.	Spanish Pueblo and Mexican Capital, 1769-1849	9
II.	Yankee Boomtown, 1850-1899	25
III.	Oil and Water, 1900-1909	51
IV.	Stars over Otistown, 1910-1919	71
V.	The Dizzy Decade, 1920-1929	87
VI.	Depression and "A Dream of Empire", 1930-1939	109
VII.	War and Peace, 1940-1949	129
VIII.	Getting Into the Big Leagues, 1950-1959	147
IX.	Divide and Conquer, 1960-1969	161
X.	Present Indicative, 1970-1980	177
XI.	Los Angeles Miscellany	200
	Sources	217
	Index	225

The horse, the trolley car and the automobile meet in the stately Spring Street cañon, circa 1910.

Chapter 1

Spanish Pueblo, Mexican Capital 1769-1849

"In the hands of an enterprising people, what a country this might be!"
—RICHARD HENRY DANA, 1840

ANGELINOS, as all the world knows, are conceived on freeway off-ramps, born in drive-in maternity clinics, reared on surfboards and, at an advanced age, laid to rest in the same cemetery where they got married. The most American of all American cities is also the most maligned. It has become a universal metaphor for urban sprawl, congested traffic and polluted air, but newcomers keep pouring in, while myth-makers keep picturing it as a semi tropical adaptation of Sodom and Cedar Rapids.

"Some Americans despise Los Angeles, just as some Europeans despise America, and for the same reason," columnist George F. Will once pointed out. "Los Angeles, like America, like freedom applied, is strong medicine—an untidy jumble of human diversity and perversity."

The city is a grab bag ("a container filled with articles, such as party gifts, to be drawn sight unseen"). One Angelino reaches in and pulls out a hit record, another draws a Nobel Prize or a diploma as an ordained minister of the Church of the Open Palm. If there is one thing they all share, it is faith in the existence of those party gifts snuggled somewhere amidst the grab bag's junk.

"In Los Angeles, you never feel weird or out of place," a high school student wrote some years ago, expressing a sentiment equally acceptable to the city's detractors who regard it as a vast unfenced asylum for the earth's incurable misfits, and to its apologists who delight in its traditional tolerance of free and independent spirits.

The Central City is like a schoolroom blackboard, changing from class to class. Successive waves of outlanders have attacked it with an eraser in one hand, chalk in the other, rubbing out brush huts and putting up adobe houses, and then leveling the adobes to make way for the red-brick shops and office buildings of Yankee entrepreneurs. The ebullient 1920s scrawled a self-portrait across the sky in the form of the black-and-gold Richfield building. The 1970s erased it and ran up the twin fifty-two-story towers of the Atlantic Richfield Plaza.

"Progress and improvement have this week laid their relentless hands upon one of the old and very familiar landmarks of the city," the Los Angeles *Star* reported September 11, 1869, when wrecking crews tore into the tile-roofed adobe mansion of the late Don José Antonio Carrillo to clear space for what was to become a new Plaza landmark, the Pico House. Twenty-odd years later, when the city was creeping south on Spring and Broadway, and west on Fifth and Sixth Streets, the hotel was referred to in the public prints as "a monument of the past."

"What changes do you expect to see in the city during the next five years?" Mayor Tom Bradley was asked at a 1980 breakfast meeting of his west-side constituents.

"Would you settle for the next five minutes?" he countered.

The towers of the city's downtown skyline cast their shadows across a bustling plain where an Indian village, a Spanish colonial settlement, a Mexican provincial capital and a Yankee boomtown lie buried beneath the same asphalt blanket. Civil servants and elderly derelicts, young Chicanos and middle-aged Nisei scurry through glass-and-granite canyons where long-haired aborigines once hunted antelope and bearded pioneers pruned their vineyards with the steel springs of old beaver traps.

New England merchants had been packing their sons off to Harvard College for more than a hundred years before aboriginal Angelinos got their first glimpse of civilization in the summer of 1769, when a party of Spaniards pitched camp on a riverbank near what is now the North Broadway entrance to Elysian Park. A small delegation of naked native villagers dropped by with gifts of seeds and woven baskets, along with some samples of the local currency, strings of beads made of shells.

"We gave them a little tobacco and glass beads, and they went away well pleased," a forty-eight-year-old Franciscan priest, Juan Crespi, observed in his diary and, despite "three consecutive earthquakes in the afternoon and night," he noted that "this delightful place among the trees on the river" had "all the requisites for a large settlement."

Some ten million men, women and children now live within a couple of hours by car from the Spanish campsite. Like the aborigines who clustered together in small, self-sufficient villages, present-day Angelinos make their home in suburban enclaves—Hollywood, Bel-Air, Sherman Oaks, Encino, Pacific Palisades, Brentwood, Watts, San Pedro—all of which are part of a city spread over 464 square miles and more populous than half of the union's fifty states.

The aboriginal Angelino took his ease in the village sweathouse, where he gossiped and gambled on a game he called *churchurki* (guessing which hand held a small piece of bone or wood). The modern Angelino climbs into a hot tub with a chilled wine and a warm friend, and out of this serenity come new stories for the world's screens, new songs for its rock groups, new sportswear for its leisure hours.

"We have our surf, and sand, our sun, our junk food, and one another," says G. Merle Bergman, a Los Angeles attorney, "and we can run barefoot through life, enjoying every blessed wasted moment of it."

* * *

The first Angelinos were a short, stocky breed who lived in brush huts and bartered their seeds and deerskins for the fish and soapstone pots of coastal villagers. They worked hard at what had to be done, the women pounding acorns and weaving baskets, the men stringing bows and flaking arrow points of flint or volcanic glass. When there was no work to be done, the women chattered and kept an eye on the children while the men lolled about the *temescal*, a sweathouse where they swapped stories, sang, boasted and played *churchurki*.

They rarely went to war, and when they did, it was not to seize a neighbor's land but to take vengeance for such offenses against their village as the theft of a woman or the practice of harmful wizardry. They regarded their medicine men as sorcerers and seers, who could not only cure diseases but create them as well. These shamans could also predict the future and produce rain. Their fees were considered exorbitant, but if their treatment failed to effect a cure, the payment was returned, and if they continued to practice bad medicine, they ran the risk of being put to death by the arrows of a dead patient's grief-stricken relatives.

The chief of a village was permitted two or three wives; lesser men made do with one woman. If she took a lover, her husband had the right to maim or kill her, but ordinarily he simply moved in with the lover's wife. Once married, a woman never visited her relatives again. They were free to call on her, however, and if she complained of being ill-treated, they could return her marriage settlement and deliver her into the hands of a more satisfactory mate.

As people who believed they had once been animals, they took no creature's life wantonly. The porpoise was held in high regard because it went about the world making sure that all was well. The eagle had once been the chief of a large tribe. Crows told them when strangers were coming, owls when death was near. They had no belief in resurrection and, until the blue-eyed strangers came among them, they had never conceived the idea of hell.

Qua-o-ar had formed their world from chaos and placed it on the shoulders of seven giants whose restlessness caused the earth to tremble at times. The god was held in such awe that his name could only be whispered and was never to be taken in vain. When it was necessary to speak of their creator, the villagers substituted the name, Y-yo-ha-rivg-nain (Giver of Life). Their religious faith was summed up in the words, *Tavi heterkrinuj atavin tuvangnar* (God has placed the whole world).

* * *

Although Spaniards had embarked on the conquest of Mexico in 1519, two hundred and fifty years slipped by before they ventured north into the heathen wilderness of what now constitutes the state of California. Juan Rodríguez Cabrillo sailed along its coast in 1542 and sixty years later Sebastián Vizcaíno entered San Diego Bay, but not until 1769 did the Spaniards get around to launching a land expedition north of the port of San Diego, the boundary between the sparsely settled peninsula of Baja (Lower) California and the unexplored territory of Alta (Upper) California.*

Led by the Spanish Governor of the Californias, Don Gaspar de Portolá, the expedition left San Diego July 14, heading for

* The two Californias were partitioned by decree of the King of Spain in 1804, with Monterey designated the capital of Alta California.

The flat-roofed adobe village has begun to spread out toward the mountains by the 1870s.

Monterey Bay and hoping to find suitable mission sites along the way. Nearly a hundred years later, in the early 1850s, the reaction of aboriginal Angelinos to the arrival of the strangers was described by Hugo Reid, a Scotsman who, in 1835, was given official permission to marry a remarkable young woman of Indian birth, Victoria Bartoloméa Comecrabit.

"The Indians were sadly afraid when they saw the Spaniards coming on horseback," he wrote. "Thinking them gods, the women ran to the brush, and hid themselves, while the men put out the fires in their huts. They remained still more impressed with this idea, when they saw one of the guests take a flint, strike a fire and commence smoking, never having seen it produced in this simple manner before.

"An occurrence however soon convinced them that their strange visitors were, like themselves, mortals, for one of the Spaniards leveled his musket at a bird and killed it. Although greatly terrified at the report of the piece, yet the effect it produced of taking life, led them to reason, and deduce the impossibility of the 'Giver of Life' to murder animals, as they themselves did with bows and arrows. They consequently put them down as human beings, of a nasty white color, and having ugly blue eyes!"

As the Spaniards rode west along what was to become Wilshire Boulevard's Miracle Mile, they spotted "some large marshes of a certain substance like pitch; they were boiling and bubbling." Coming upon the pits of *brea* (tar) after having been jolted by half a dozen earthquakes in the last two days, the visitors wondered if this black substance had caused the temblors, but, as any child in the nearby village of Yangna could have explained, the earthquakes had been brought about by the giants who bore the world's weight on their shoulders.

The Spaniards came back two years later and, on September 8, 1771, founded the Mission San Gabriel Arcangel about nine miles northeast of the river they called the Porciúncula. Another ten years went by before they staked out the plaza for a pueblo on the west bank of the river. The Alta California pueblos were farming

Courtesy Security Pacific Bank

To still their historic fear of thirst, Angelinos store river water in a brick reservoir in the Plaza.

communities designed to provide the food and fiber Spain's priests and soldiers needed to sustain them in their efforts to convert the "Gentiles," as the natives were called, and at the same time discourage Russia and England from encroaching on the undeveloped frontier of New Spain.

The settlers who agreed to try their luck in the Porciúncula pueblo were rounded up in the Mexican provinces of Sonora and Sinaloa. The recruiting agent had been instructed to seek out working class family men who were "healthy, robust and without known vice," because they would be "situated in the midst of a numerous population of Gentiles, docile and without malice but susceptible, like all Indians, to the first impressions of good or bad example set by the Spaniards who settle among them aiming to civilize them...."

* * *

On September 4, 1781, after having been quarantined about three miles south of Mission San Gabriel because of exposure to smallpox on their arduous, seven-month journey, the *vecinos pobladores* (village settlers) set out with their horses and mules to take possession of the land they had been promised. Each of the eleven family heads was entitled to a fifty-by-one-hundred-foot lot facing the Plaza and to seven acres of farmland. They were also expected to share in the work of cultivating the *propios* (municipal lands) and the *realengos* (royal lands). The king's acreage would later blossom forth as Boyle Heights.

The settlers followed a dusty old Indian trail (now Mission Road), cut across a stretch of wild country destined to make way for the city of Alhambra and probably forded the Porciúncula near what was to become Aliso Street. Its name derived from the giant sycamore which a hundred years later shaded a local brewery, just as—according to legend—it had once shaded the council of the first Angelinos.

Most of the newcomers, the Indians would have noted, were

dark-skinned and dark-eyed. Only two of the forty-four settlers claimed to be Spaniards. The rest were Indians, Negroes and *mestizos* (of mixed ancestry). The blood of Africa flowed in the veins of twenty-six *pobladores*. Spanish law had always made it easy for black bondsmen to buy their freedom in New Spain, and custom had raised no barriers to intermarriage.

The oldest settler was Basilio Rosas, a sixty-seven-year-old Indian who had made the difficult journey across deserts and mountains with his mulatto wife and six children. One of the boys, twelve-year-old José Carlos, would later marry a native girl from Yangna (or "Yabit," as the San Gabriel missionaries called it) and long afterwards, when the pueblo celebrated the one hundred and fiftieth anniversary of its founding, their descendants in San Gabriel would have their pictures in the paper.

No eyewitness account of the pueblo's founding has ever turned up (none of the founding fathers could read and write), but myth-makers have cloaked the day's events in suitable splendor, depicting Governor Felipe de Neve on horseback at the head of a procession of priests, soldiers, settlers and converted Indians. By the start of the twentieth century the ceremony was thought to be "probably the most extensive and the most impressive that was ever held over the founding of an American city."

It is doubtful, however, that the California Governor was on hand (he hadn't shown up for the founding of San José in 1777) or that priests from Mission San Gabriel made much of a fuss over this secular intrusion on their authority. A grey-robed friar may have mumbled a blessing and the corporal in command of the three soldiers escorting the colonists may have planted the flag of Spain in the Plaza, but the *pobladores* were probably much too busy with their makeshift wickiups to bother with ceremony.

While the women fetched water from the river to cook the evening's supper, the older boys would be taking care of the livestock and the girls would be quieting baby brothers and sisters (and flirting with the soldiers). In the darkness that night, hunkering into the bare ground like savages, some of the heads of the pueblo's first families must have had misgivings about their decision to plow and plant this remote rim of Christendom the Spaniards had named *El Pueblo de la Reina de los Angeles* (The Town of the Queen of the Angels).*

* * *

On El Pueblo's fifth anniversary, when the settlers took title to their land by scratching an X on a document held out to them by the governor's representative, José Argüello, only eight of the founding fathers were on hand. Three had been expelled as "useless." The granddaughter of one of the rejects, a fifty-three-year-old black tailor named Luis Quintero, ended up owning a 4,500-acre ranch, Rodeo de las Aguas (Meeting of the Waters), which eventually fell into the hands of a Yankee subdivider who dubbed it Beverly Hills.

José Sinova, who had lived in Alta California for some years, joined the eight remaining settlers at the September 4, 1786 ceremony and received a deed to his land and a branding iron for his cattle. Two sons of old Basilio Rosas came of age and they, too, were granted their property rights as *pobladores*. Meanwhile, little girls were growing up and marrying young soldiers, and old frontier veterans with no homes to go back to were riding into town to live out their lives in a warm, agreeable place where there was food to eat, wine to drink and ears to bend with stories of the good old days.

During its first ten years the settlement gained twenty families among them men with such now familiar names as Pico, Sepulveda, Figueroa and Soto. The climate was so salubrious that nine of the town's eighty adults claimed to have passed their ninetieth birthday. By the turn of the century some thirty one-story adobe houses, most of them with only a single windowless, dirt-floored room, were clustered around the Plaza, and the town was taking on the look of a retirement village for old soldiers, a few of whom had been rewarded with vast grants of land. The

---

* For years antiquarians argued about the pueblo's correct title. Theodore E. Treutlein disposed of the controversy in the Spring, 1973, issue of the *Southern California Quarterly*.

neighboring hills were dotted with their cattle.

Juan José Domínguez, a sixty-five-year-old bachelor veteran of the Portolá expedition built a corral for his herd on what came to be known as Rancho San Pedro. In the same year, 1784, José María Verdugo was given the grasslands now occupied by Glendale and part of Burbank. Manuel Pérez Nieto's vast acreage was later carved into a number of cities, including Long Beach.

Although the missionaries at San Gabriel complained of the town's preoccupation with fast horses, strong drink and loose women, the settlers managed to produce more grain, cattle, horses and sheep than any other community in Alta California. They were so far removed from the historic turmoil of the Atlantic seaboard that George Washington had been in his tomb nearly three years before they saw a ship from the United States. The arrival of the *Lelia Bird* in 1803 touched off a brisk commerce in the smuggling of otter skins and, later on, of bullock hides and tallow.

El Pueblo's first foreigner, José Antonio Rocha, arrived from Portugal in 1815 and ran up an imposing home which was later to serve as the town's first city hall. The first Angelinos from the United States were two pirates who came ashore in 1818 and promptly mended their ways. One was a black buccaneer, Thomas Fisher, who seems to have vanished some years later in the gold rush. The other was a blonde blue-eyed Bostonian, Joseph Chapman. His home town and the republic its rebels had helped bring into being were so remote from his new Spanish-speaking neighbors that they called him *El Ingles* (The Englishman).

* * *

In the spring of 1822 word reached El Pueblo that Mexico had won its independence from Spain. California was now Mexican territory, with its capital at Monterey. Angelinos dutifully changed the flag flying above the Plaza, replacing the Spanish lion with the Mexican serpent, and went on about their affairs.

Some months later, in December, they dedicated the church it had taken them more than forty years to build. It faced the new Plaza, which had been shifted to its present location in 1818, reversing the direction of the town's growth. Instead of moving north, it had begun inching south.

Two enterprising Yanquis, John Temple and George Rice, opened the town's first general merchandise store in 1828 on the southern edge of town, the site of the present Federal Building at the corner of Temple and Main. Temple bought out his partner and by 1836, according to the census figures for the Los Angeles district, he had a potential market of 2,228 customers, including the town's 250 women, 15 of whom were identified professionally by the initials, "M.V." *(Mala Vida*—Bad Life).

Twenty-nine of the area's fifty foreigners (other than Spaniards) hailed from the United States. Their ranks included not only Don Juan Temple but also Abel Stearns, another New England hustler. He trafficked in hides and wine, did a little smuggling on the side, and ended up as Southern California's wealthiest landowner. He was so homely his neighbors dubbed him *Cara de Caballo* (Horseface), but in 1841, at the age of forty-three, he picked off the city's prize beauty, his friend Juan Bandini's fourteen-year-old daughter, Arcadia, and installed her in an adobe mansion on what is now the southeast corner of Main and Arcadia Streets.

Thanks to José Antonio Carrillo, the hulking, swaggering plotter of revolutions who dominated Southern California politics for a quarter of a century, the town was officially declared a *ciudad* (city) in 1835 and was also designated the capital of the territory. Mexican governors, however, refused to exchange the civilized amenities of Monterey for the crudities of an overgrown village bursting with saloons, bordellos and gambling dens, but with no public buildings fit to house the government.

The raunchy reputation of the capital in name only spread to England in the 1840s when a traveler described it as a "den of thieves" teeming with "the lowest drunkards and gamblers of the country." The narrow, crooked streets meandering off from the Plaza were dusty in summer, muddy in winter, unrelieved by sidewalks or shade trees. To a disgusted local official, the gloomy, clay-colored house fronts of El Pueblo suggested "the catacombs of ancient Rome more than the habitation of a free people."

Like the Spanish explorers in the Portolá party who had been struck with wonder at the sight of the black, bubbling marshes of *brea* west of the river, nineteenth-century visitors were awed by the pits and impressed by the ingenious use the townspeople made of the stuff. They smeared it on their flat roofs to keep out the rain. In hot weather the tar melted and trickled down the adobe walls, forming sticky pools in the unpaved streets.

Indians were hired for a pittance to haul the *brea* in ox-drawn carts. They also made the adobe bricks, built the houses, planted the corn, crushed the grapes, ground the flour, baked the bread, cradled the babies, dug the graves, sewed the ball gowns, polished the family silver, swept the Plaza and hauled the bullock hides to San Pedro.

With native labor so cheap and abundant, Angelinos were inclined to idleness and self-indulgence, much to the disgust of the first Puritanical New Englanders to look in on them. The ladies were free to dance and flirt the night away, sleep all morning and then stroll down to Hugo Reid's new *tienda* on the Plaza to fondle a fresh shipment of silk *rebozos* from Acapulco or dining room chairs from Boston. The men never thought of walking anywhere. Even to cross the Plaza, they hopped on a horse. They were often in wine and, when the cards were running against them, in debt as well.

"In the hands of an enterprising people, what a country this might be," mused Richard Henry Dana in *Two Years Before the Mast*, an 1840 best seller. The sentiment was echoed by a Yankee trader in a letter to the folks back home: "All California wants to make it the first country in the world is about

10,000 New England farmers, with their families, churches and schools."

* * *

When Sir George Simpson passed through California on his 1841 trip around the world, he found its trade in the hands of foreigners, most of them from the United States. Five years later, after gringos had maneuvered Texas into the Union and California seemed manifestly destined to follow suit, an often-quoted speech attributed to Governor Pío Pico warned Californians against the "hordes of Yankee emigrants" swarming across the province.

"They are cultivating farms, establishing vineyards, erecting mills, sawing up lumber, building workshops, and doing a thousand other things which seem natural to them, but which Californians neglect or despise. What then are we to do? Shall we remain supine, while these daring strangers are overrunning our fertile plains, and gradually outnumbering and displacing us? Shall these incursions go on unchecked, until we shall become strangers in our own land?"

Pico urged secession from "the mock republic of Mexico" and annexation with France or England, the "two great powers in Europe which seem destined to divide between them the unappropriated countries of the world." Protected by the ships and soldiers of either country, the Governor argued, Californians would once again be able to "go quietly to their ranchos, and live there as of yore, leading a merry and thoughtless life, untroubled by politics or cares of state."

Never again would Californians live so merrily and so free of political cares, and never would their guests be given quite the same hospitality. As H. H. Bancroft noted, "a person could travel from San Diego to Sonoma without a coin in his pocket, and never want for a roof to cover him, a bed to sleep on, food to eat, and even tobacco to smoke." Their hosts gave what others sold. Proud, generous, vulnerable, they were no more capable of dealing with the Yanqui's dollar than the Indians had been prepared to deal with the Spaniard's musket and cross.

Americans led by Major John C. Frémont and Commodore Robert F. Stockton marched on Los Angeles in the summer of 1846 and entered the city August 13 without firing a shot. When they went north a few weeks later, they left an officious American officer and fifty men behind to keep an eye on the city. Rebellious Angelinos sent him packing, but four months later, on January 18, 1847, he returned with reinforcements. The Stars and Stripes went back up over the city and a band played in the Plaza while Commodore Stockton relaxed in the adobe home of Doña Encarnación Ávila on what is now Olvera Street.

"As the savages faded before the superior Mexicans, so faded the Mexicans before the superior Americans," Bancroft wrote. One of the few Indians to live to see the dawn of the twentieth century summed it up for his people in less than a dozen words: "When Indians died, the villages ended. We, all the people, ended."

Chapter 2

Yankee Boomtown
1850–1899

"Time, flood, and the hated gringos have long since obliterated all ancient landmarks and boundaries of the old pueblos."

—J.M. GUINN, 1895

THE CITY FATHERS, staring into a bare municipal cupboard in the summer of 1849, decided to go into the real estate business, but before they could sell any part of the pueblo's Spanish land grant, an area of four square leagues (17,172.37 acres) measured "one league to each wind" from the front door of the Plaza Church, they had to have a survey of their royal patrimony.* The assignment went to a thirty-year-old West Pointer, Lieutenant Edward Otho Cresap Ord, grandson of George I of England and his morganatic

* The Spanish league was 2.6 miles.

Courtesy Security Pacific Bank

The dusty commercial establishments of South Main Street bake in the summer sun of the 1880s.

wife, Maria Anne Fitzherbert.

The young officer shrewdly offered to take half of his fee in land, but had to settle for cash. The *ayuntamiento* (city council) was looking ahead to the "not improbable" day when the city's population would have soared to 5,000 and the vacant lots the lieutenant had his eye on might be worth more than the $3,000 he charged for preparing the city's first detailed map.

"We commenced last Monday," Ord's assistant, William Rich Hutton, wrote on Sunday, July 29, "& have gone from the church to the last house on the main street, about 1¼ miles."

In the gamey native quarter north of the Plaza Church, where life was cheap and, on Saturday night, likely to end abruptly, Ord showed *Calle de Eternidad* crossing *Calle de Las Virgenes* on its way to the cemetery. For a later generation of Angelinos, Eternity Street was known as Buena Vista. It is now North Broadway. The Street of the Virgins, noted in its heyday less for its virtue than for its venery, appears on current maps as Alpine Street.

The last numbered street to the south was Eighth, but Ord's map took note of unnamed east-west streets as far out in the country as present-day Pico Boulevard. The north-south streets west of Main were *Primavera* (Spring), *Fortin* (Fort, now Broadway), *Loma* (Hill), *Aceituna* (Olive), *Caridad* (now Grand), *Esperanzas* (Hope), *Flores* (Flower) and *Calle de Los Chapules* (Street of the Grasshoppers, now Figueroa).

Grasshopper Street, at the time of the American occupation, marked the western border of the pueblo. In dry years, grasshoppers left the *cienegas* (swamps) around what is now Marina del Rey and swarmed across the parched landscape looking for vegetation to feed on. Once they came into view above *Calle de Los Chapules*, the grapegrowers knew that their vineyards in the east end of town would be devastated. They kept a wary eye on the skies above Grasshopper Street.

Ord delivered his map, or as he called it, his "Plan de La Ciudad de Los Angeles," in mid-September and the first auction was held on November 7. Fifty-four lots were sold at prices ranging from $50 to $200. Lots in the older part of town, north of the Plaza, brought less than those in the "lower district," the municipal acreage bounded by Second and Fourth, Spring and Hill. They city was being pushed farther and farther away from its birthplace.

"An antiquated, dilapidated air pervades all," John W. Audubon noted in his western journal in 1849, "but Americans are pouring in, and in a few years will make a beautiful place of it . . . ."
In the mining towns up north claim-jumpers and camp-followers were gorging on Southern California beef in the 1850s, while Angelinos built their first school "out in the country" on the northeast corner of Second and Spring, gulped their first oysters, imported their first bees, attended their first Protestant service and fired their first bricks in a kiln on the west side of Fort Street (Broadway) south of Second.

"But one solitary brick structure reared its walls within the precincts of the Angel city, three or four wooden tenements and the balance were adobe houses," a visiting editor noted in 1853.

As the decade drew to a close, more than thirty brick buildings went up in a single year, the most imposing of which was Abel Stearns' two-story Arcadia Block on the corner of Los Angeles and Arcadia Streets. Don Abel had also set the town's tongues to wagging by sending to Boston for the first carriage to be seen in Los Angeles. Gossips insisted the old man did it to please his young wife. Wives of lesser men still went about in *carretas*, lumbering carts mounted above two solid wheels of sawed-off logs.

Angelinos, as mirrored in the pages of the *Star*, worried about law and murder ("Crime is perpetrated openly and with impunity"), discussed the feasibility of lighting the city with gas ("Our streets will become safe and pleasant for an evening stroll"), assembled at the Mechanics' Institute to debate the question: "Should Capital Punishment Be Abolished?" and sought to preserve pedestrians as an endangered species by declaring it illegal "for any person to ride any mule, horse or other animal within the city limits at a furious rate."

"Los Angeles, prosperous, growing," Richard Henry Dana jotted down in his journal when he revisited the city in the summer of 1859.

The Mexican provincial capital had become so Americanized that it outlawed bullfighting in 1860 and formed a club "for the promotion of the manly art of base ball playing." It warmed the *Star's* Democratic, Lincoln-hating heart to see local schoolboys aping their elders by spending "their play hours in this healthy recreation." In their fathers' day, they would have been roping and breaking wild horses, showing off their mastery of the rawhide rope they called a *reata*.

The north end of town, however, held fast against change. It was still a squat, adobe Mexican village, teeming with goats, chickens and children. So many of the *paisanos* hailed from Sonora that the *barrio* was called Sonora Town. While the Plaza's landed gentry went its own aristocratic way and south side Yankees busied themselves with commerce, the men of Sonora Town found what work they could, bet on cards and cockfights, drank their one-bit wine and gave the community a reputation for drunken and often fatal quarrels.

"Last Sunday night was a brisk night for killing," reported the *Southern Californian* on March 5, 1855. "Four men were shot and several were wounded in shooting frays."

Much of the city's mayhem took place in an alley which has long since been swallowed up by the 400 block of North Los Angeles Street. One morning in 1832, so the story goes, Don José Antonio Carrillo posted a sign, *Calle de Los Negros* (Street of the Blacks) at each end of the narrow, block-long alley southeast of the Plaza owned and occupied by Los Negros, as all dark-skinned Angelinos were called at that time.

The name stuck for more than forty years, but in common usage the 500-foot strip of adobe brothels, saloons and tenements was referred to as Negro, or more often, Nigger Alley. In a community which has never been known to back off from the use of a superlative, it was called "the wickedest street on earth." At one time it was averaging a homicide a day, not counting Indians.

The criminal violence of Nigger Alley was as effective as a firing squad in destroying the descendants of the aboriginal Angelinos. After the missions were reduced to the status of parish churches by secularization in the 1830s, the Indians had found themselves in a cultural limbo, cut off from the institutionalized life of the missions, unable to go back to their old ways or to cope with the new. They had turned to thievery and prostitution to support their addiction to *aguardiente*, a raw native brandy which served as a blindfold while their unpronounced sentence of death was being carried out.

"The brute upshot of missionization, in spite of its kindly flavor and humanitarian roots," A.L. Kroeber observed, "was only one thing: death."

The Americans speeded up the genocidal process by rebuilding El Pueblo with slave labor. On Saturday and Sunday, when Indian field hands had drunk up their week's pay, they were arrested and herded into a corral where, on Monday morning, they were auctioned off to the highest bidders by order of the city council. Bids ran from $1 to $3 with the city treasury getting two-thirds of the take. The rest went to the Indians, enabling them to get sufficently drunk the following week end to ensure their arrest and their return to the auction block.

"The effect on the individual Indian was to destroy him in one year, or two, or three years," W.W. Robinson wrote. "So passed from the scene the descendants of those friendly, brown-skinned people who had come timidly out of their villages in the Los Angeles and surrounding areas to greet the first Spanish explorers with offers of seeds and shell beads."

* * *

On Christmas Eve, 1861, it started to rain and, with two slight interruptions, it lasted for thirty days. The city's new public water

From Fort Moore Hill oldtimers watch the Yankee city move south, farther and farther from its Plaza birthplace.

Courtesy Security Pacific Bank

In the native quarter north of the Plaza, shaded by pepper trees, Sonora Town holds out against change.

system collapsed. Adobe walls crumbled. Vineyards and orchards were swept away. Firewood stacked in the cañons was carried out to sea. Main Street shopkeepers stood in water waistdeep, struggling to save their merchandise.

By spring, however, the weather was delightful and, the *News* observed, the hills were "covered with a luxuriant growth of grass." Having dug themselves out from the mud and debris, Angelinos took up football, built a brick sewer, argued slavery and secession, and suddenly found themselves up against a smallpox epidemic. It started among the Indians in November, 1862, and spread quickly, taking a particularly cruel toll in Sonora Town. Yellow flags marked the stricken adobes and deaths were so frequent that the city fathers put a stop to ringing the Plaza Church bells for the souls of the departed.

A curse seemed to have been laid upon the land when the plague, in 1864, gave way to drought, and lean, long-horned cattle were staggering across the lion-colored hills, dying in dusty creekbeds. Finally, in mid-November, 1865, the rains returned and the *News* rejoiced at the beauty of the countryside ("one vast meadow"). With the end of the drought came the end of the pastoral age. The rancheros had been done in by depressed cattle prices, withered grass, delinquent tax bills and unpaid loans.

The gracious hospitable Dons had never given much thought to maps and documents establishing ownership of land that everybody knew was theirs until they had to defend their Spanish and Mexican grants in Yanqui courts. They were incapable of coping with the gringo's legalisms (not to mention the interest rates on what many of them had taken to be a neighbor's friendly loan). Their day was done; the day of the developer was at hand.

"Many of the largest grants of land in the county have been subdivided and thrown into market," the *News* reported in 1868 and six years later the *Star* beamed approvingly at the disappearance of the city's adobe houses, which "do well enough for a country where all out of doors is not considered too much for a melon-patch, but in a community of Anglo-Saxons, where men institute expensive lawsuits to establish the right to possession and ownership of three inches, or even one inch, of frontage, walls two or three feet thick 'won't pay.' "

* * *

On the epoch-making spring day of May 10, 1869, when San Francisco was linked with the eastern seaboard by the golden spike driven into the ground at Promontory Point, Utah, to mark completion of the country's first transcontinental railroad, Angelinos were still depending on horses, mules and oxen to carry their guests and their grapes, wine, oranges, lemons, grain and wool between the city and its port, but Phineas Banning, whose stagecoaches and freight wagons had been making the Los Angeles-San Pedro run for years, was about to propel the community's archaic transportation industry into the nineteenth century.

After getting himself elected to the State Senate, he pushed through two railroad bills authorizing the county and city of Los Angeles to subscribe $225,000 in capital stock. The bills were signed by the Governor on February 1, 1868. The scheme would bankrupt local government, diehards insisted, but when the proposal was placed on the ballot the following month, a majority of the electorate opted for the railroad. Developers tumbled over one another bidding up the price of urban real estate.

"During the past week," the *News* reported, "land situated two miles from the Plaza sold for $80 per acre that could have been bought one year ago for $14 per acre. Nearer the business center, lots one hundred and twenty feet front are now selling for $1,000 which could be purchased three months ago for $300."

The first railroad south of the Tehachapis formally opened on the morning of October 26, 1869. A train left the new Los Angeles depot on the southwest corner of Alameda and Commercial Streets at nine o'clock and pulled into Wilmington within the hour. The harbor area depot was located on a fifteen-acre tract Senator Banning had parted with for a consideration of $39,000.

The Senator had also won the contract to build the tracks at a cost of $19,000 per mile.

* * *

When Spain staked its claim to California, the king's priests and soldiers built a string of missions and presidios along a royal highway. When the Southern Pacific staked its claim to the state a hundred years later, it built a string of railroad depots* designed not only to accommodate passengers and freight, but also to remind the town that it owed its prosperity, perhaps even its existence, to what Californians called "The Octopus."

The Octopus wriggled south from San Francisco, gathering farm towns into its steel tentacles. If a town resisted its demands, it was denied rail service, and then left to wither and die. While SP construction crews ran up new depots in the center of communities willing to knuckle under, SP land agents were fanning out over the San Joaquin Valley creating such new towns as Modesto, Merced and Fresno. When The Octopus crawled to the Tehachapis, it paused, giving Los Angeles time to consider its terms.

Along with the usual right-of-way, it demanded a chunk of cash, sixty acres in the middle of the city for a depot and control of the Los Angeles & San Pedro Railroad. Angelinos fumed for a year and finally, in 1872, gave in. Four years later, on September 5, the San Francisco-to-Los Angeles track was joined at Lang's Station in Soledad Cañon near Newhall.

The Octopus also took over the Los Angeles & Independence Railroad, which carried young lovers out to the beach at Santa Monica and gave local merchants, manufacturers, farmers and winegrowers a harbor closer to San Francisco than San Pedro. Once it acquired the line, the SP razed its wooden depot on San Pedro Street. The entrance had been flanked by the two bronze sphinxes pictured in contemporary annals as being "of heroic size and rather imposing demeanor." They disappeared for a while,

---

* "*Depot* is very commonly used instead of station, and in many places the latter word, when used alone, means police-station"—*Baedeker's United States, 1909.*

only to be resurrected in the front yard of Cora Phillips' sporting house on Alameda Street, a block or so south of the SP depot.

* * *

With the completion of the transcontinental railroad, the state's labor market was overrun by Chinese, many of whom had originally come to California in search of gold. While politicians competed for the workingman's vote by trying to outdo one another in trumpeting their dislike and distrust of the "heathen Chinee," some of the Orientals drifted away from the industrial north to the agricultural south, where they were not competing with Caucasians when they opened wash-houses in Los Angeles, peddled vegetables and gradually ousted Indians and Negroes from suburban kitchens.

By 1870 there were 172 Chinese in the city, dozens of them concentrated in the adobe hovels of Nigger Alley where, on the evening of October 26, 1871, a white man stopped a Chinese bullet while trying to help a policeman break up an altercation between two rival tongs. The death of Robert Thompson in a Main Street drug store touched off a five-hour orgy of shooting, stabbing, hanging and looting that left nineteen Chinese dead.

Next morning when the bodies were laid out in double rows on the northern side of the jail, where City Hall now stands, rope still trailed from some of the broken necks. The mob had torn the trousers from the body of Chinatown's highly respected doctor, Chee Long Tong, to get at the money in his pockets and had hacked the ring finger from another corpse. With one exception, eyewitnesses told a newspaper reporter, none of the dead men had been guilty of any wrongdoing.

The November term grand jury called 111 witnesses, most of whom showed "a blamable reluctance" to tell what they knew of the "crimes which must cause christianity to weep, civilization to blush, and humanity to mourn." The jurors came to the "painful conclusion" that law enforcement officers had been "deplorably inefficient," having made no attempt "to arrest any of those, who, in their presence were openly, and grossly, violating the law, even to the taking of human life."

The evidence suggested to the jurors that "a great majority of those who witnessed the sad spectacles of that night, instead of being a blood-thirsty mob, having possession of the city, or any part of it, trampling law and order under foot, were unwilling witnesses, anxious to prevent the revolting scenes that were passing before their eyes and would, quickly and cheerfully, have prevented, or put an end to the anarchy, if any resolute and energetic man, clothed with authority, and with an average share of ability and judgment, had placed himself at their head, and in a proper manner directed their efforts."

Many of the defendants, seeking to justify their criminal conduct, testified that they had merely carried out orders given them by law enforcement officers on the scene. "There is ground to suspect that improper instructions were given by officers," the grand jury report acknowledged, but nearly a hundred years before the Nuremberg trials and the My Lai massacre, the jurors pointed out that "the orders of an officer are no excuse for the commission of a criminal act."

"The jury handed in forty-nine indictments, twenty-five of which are for the crime of murder and accessories," the *Star* reported.* Seven men were found guilty and given sentences of from two to six years. The judge who presided over the trials was Robert M. Widney, one of the founders of the University of Southern California. New to the bench, Judge Widney was not sufficiently steeped in the law's subtleties to spot a fatal defect in the indictments. The convictions were reversed on appeal and the seven men set free.

Under state law, Chinese were not permitted to testify in matters involving Caucasians at the time of the Nigger Alley massacre. When the law was quietly done away with in 1873, Chinese merchants sued the city for its negligence in permitting a mob to pillage their shops. The grand jury, it would appear, had paved

* In accounts of the Chinese Massacre, the number of indictments varies widely. The late Paul M. DeFalla's study of the case led him to conclude that twenty-three men were indicted, but two were never brought to court.

Courtesy Security Pacific Bank

A busy day in the San Fernando Valley.

the way for the plaintiffs by calling attention to the deplorable inefficiency of local authorities, but the inscrutable Occidentals sitting on the state's highest tribunal ruled against the Chinese merchants because of their failure "to summon the police before the shooting commenced."

* * *

Easterners discovered Los Angeles in 1871 when its slaughter of the Chinese hit the front pages of their newspapers and its grapes went on exhibit at their state fairs ("grown under glass," snorted the disbelievers). Not knowing quite what to make of this bloodstained Eden, the venturesome travelers from the Atlantic seaboard who turned up at the Pico House clutching Spanish phrasebooks were agreeably surprised to find gas lamps and running water. John Moore, the *Star* announced, was planning to open a restaurant "on the San Francisco plan—everything to be sold by the plate."

The pueblo, in its nineties now, was trying to live down its past. "Just think of it!" the *Star* crowed at the start of 1873. "Only two drunks arrested on New Year's Day. Talk about your moral cities." The editor worried about changing mores ("The girls nowadays wear false hair, paint and—heaven knows what they won't do"), poked fun at the new blue laws ("A man may kiss his wife in his own house between two and four o'clock on Sunday morning") and grunted approval of the board of education's decisions to start expelling any youngster who came to school packing a firearm.

Visitors picked and ate a fresh orange, admired the Plaza's new fountain (a boy with a dolphin), traipsed through the east-side vineyards, made a brave stab at the Mexican cuisine, cooled their throats with the local beer, returned from a day's outing at Santa Monica clutching an abalone shell and, at dusk, watched the city's lamplighter ride through the streets from lamp to lamp. They shuddered at the filthy *zanjas* (ditches) from which the city drank and were amused, outraged or delighted when they stumbled into what they mistook for genteel boarding houses.

"There is a small street running almost parallel with and not more than a hundred blocks distant from Los Angeles Street," the *Star* noted. "There are a number of small frame houses on this thoroughfare, apparently very desirable places of residence. A stranger is looking for a house wherein to sojourn while in the city. He wants a room on some quiet street away from the bustle and noise of the business locality. He is struck with the calm and secluded appearance of the houses on this street. If he can only procure lodging here it will just suit him. While thus reflecting, lo! and behold! the wished for sign 'Furnished Rooms' meets his gaze.

"He opens the gate and walking to the door, knocks. A bashful maiden opens it, and he makes known his business. She asks him to walk in and take a seat in the parlor, while she goes to inform her 'ma.' This he does, and after waiting a few moments he is confronted by a virtuous-looking elderly female. He tells her he would like to obtain a room, and is mortified and dumbfounded with virtuous indignation when she asks him if he wishes it 'with or without ladies?' He is in a house of shame."

The city's guests went home remembering the gamecocks in the native quarter, the Chinese vegetable peddlers, the sixteen-mule teams lumbering along Los Angeles Street, the farm wagons parked around the Plaza, the new cottages clinging to the scarred cliffs in the west end and the stench of sewage so overpowering in some areas—Sixth and Main, for one—that windows couldn't be opened on hot afternoons.

On one such afternoon in September, 1872, the editor of the *Star* scrambled to the top of Telegraph Hill and, mopping his brow, looked down at the "gallant little place." His admiring gaze came to rest on the new City Park (Pershing Square). Just across the way, on Sixth Street west of Fort (Broadway), where an alleyway now provides a side-door entrance to the Los Angeles Theater, stood the front of St. Vincent's College. It was located, a guidebook noted, in "a pleasant, retired part of the city."

"Great hotels will be built in the vicinity of St. Vincent's College," the editor predicted, "and there will be the heart of the city."

* * *

"Ten years ago Los Angeles was a village," the Los Angeles *Herald* reminded its readers on Sunday, September 4, 1881, the one hundredth anniversary of the city's humble beginnings. Now, with a population hovering around 12,000, "the era of development has but just begun," the editorial continued. "Los Angeles County can support a population of one hundred thousand souls without much need of developing her latent water resources. But, as this county is certainly destined to have a population of from three hundred thousand to a million people, the onus is upon us to be up and doing."

Next day the Democratic editor received a "pleasant call" from a visiting Republican, Colonel Harrison Gray Otis, "formerly editor of the Santa Barbara *Press,* but latterly United States agent at the fur seal islands of Alaska." The Colonel was not a man to squander his vast energies on a remote, sparsely settled wilderness. He had taken a fancy to Southern California the moment he first laid eyes on it in 1874 ("fattest land I ever was in"), and now, at forty-four, he found himself infected by the *Herald's* contagious enthusiasm. A few months later he was back in town, being interviewed by a reporter from a lively new Republican paper, the *Daily Times.* He was asked to air his views on a proposal to grant Alaska territorial status.

"Useless expense," he snorted.

When he wound up his work with the fur seals the following spring, he headed back to Los Angeles, where he was greeted by the *Daily Times* as "a man of great force of character, an able writer, a good citizen, and one of the noblest works of creation— an honest man." Toward the end of July the paper announced that Colonel Otis would take over "the editorial conduct of the *Daily Times* and *Weekly Mirror.*"*

* *The Mirror*, founded in 1873, drummed up job printing business for the company.

He dropped "Daily" from the Times masthead, ordered up livelier headlines, doubled the telegraphic news coverage, made room for letters to the editor and added a column, "Political Points," which collected editorial barbs aimed at Democrats by other Republican journals. He also managed to scrape up $6,000 to buy into the company which was paying him $15 a week. A year later, in partnership with a fellow-Republican, H. H. Boyce, he bought the Times-Mirror properties.

"Los Angeles," he wrote in one of his first editorials, "is in a transition state. She has finally waked up from the dull lethargy of those old days when she was one great sheep-walk and cattle range. All she needs now is men of brawn and brains to grow up with her."

The men the Colonel counted on would vote a straight Republican ticket and stand firm against the Socialistic preachments of trade union organizers. The proprietors of the *Times*, he warned striking compositors that first summer, would never "recognize the right of persons in their employ to dictate to them the management of the office."* Los Angeles was to be an open shop city.

At the time Colonel Otis signed on as editor of the *Times*, printers were the only organized craft in town. Within the next two years, the building trades (plasterers, painters, carpenters, brick-layers) formed unions and launched a campaign for a nine-hour day. In the fall of 1886, several months after Otis had bought out his partner, Boyce hit the streets with a pro-labor paper, the *Tribune*. Union leaders were delighted with the novelty of reading full, fair coverage of their activities.

* * *

The *Times* was in its fourth year when it acquired its first city editor, Charles Fletcher Lummis, who arrived on foot from Cincinnati, Ohio, after contracting with Colonel Otis for a weekly series of letters at $5 each. He limped into San Gabriel on February 1, 1885, wearing a dusty white felt hat with a rattlesnake

---

* Otis, a member of the Typographical Union in his early days, had once quit his job because of the proprietor's mulish opposition to trade unions.

skin for a band, a coat and vest of canvas and well-worn overalls covering two pairs of pantaloons. He carried a pilgrim's staff in his right hand (his left arm, broken below the elbow, was in a bandana sling) and packed a six-shooter under his belt. The Colonel treated him to a leisurely meal under a giant grapevine and then the two men walked the remaining ten miles to Los Angeles together.

"Colonel Otis and I hit it off from the start," Lummis later recalled. "He hated anybody who was afraid of him. Because of his dominant and overbearing way a great many good people were afraid of him. One of the reasons he liked me was that I wasn't."

Before setting out in his 143-day, cross-country walk, which inspired his slogan, "See America First," Lummis had edited a four-page weekly paper in Chillicothe, Ohio, "a beautiful old town of 5,000 people." Los Angeles, he found, was "a dull little place of some 12,000 persons," with six buildings of three stories or more. The narrow, crooked streets were so muddy in the rainy season that pranksters used to sink a pole at the intersection of Spring, Main and Temple Streets and insist that a hack had just sunk from sight beneath the surface.

As the year drew to a close, the Southern Pacific and the Atchison, Topeka & Santa Fe were squaring off for a rate war that would dump thousands of new Angelinos on such booming communities as Sycamore Grove, Highland Park, Duarte, Azusa, Magnolia and Etiwanda. For a few minutes one March day in 1886 the price of a Southern Pacific ticket to Kansas City dropped to $1. Commuters saved a dollar or so by buying a ticket for the 1,700-mile trip and then hopping off the train at Newhall or Colton.

Shelter was hard to come by, as newcomers crowded into every hotel, boarding house and private home with a spare bedroom. "Landowners were repeatedly urged to build rental property," Glenn S. Dumke wrote in *The Boom of the Eighties in Southern*

Courtesy Security Pacific Bank

The Plaza, as it looked to the visitors who showed up at the Pico House in the 1870s, practicing their phrase-book Spanish.

California. "Despite agitation, they generally refused, preferring to take advantage of rising sales prices rather than risk large sums in soaring construction costs."

Two Los Angeles physicians, Walter Lindley and J. P. Widney, collaborated on a guidebook, *California of the South,* designed primarily for the health-seeker whose joints were "tortured with pains at every change in the weather." The west-bound traveler was advised to supply himself with food for four days ("canned fruit, jellies, boneless chicken, eggs, meat, butter and condensed milk"). He should also have a spirit lamp to enable him to make his own tea and coffee.

"A bottle of paregoric, a bottle of aromatic spirits of ammonia, and a flask of good whisky are all excellent things to carry in the satchel," the physicians added.

Meanwhile, the *Times* was boasting about the city's new buildings ("a magnificent courthouse, a city hall and a high school"), its public library ("excites the envy and surprise of other cities"), its two handsome theaters, Grand Opera House and Hazard's Pavilion ("a first-class show will always draw a full house in Los Angeles"), its high-masted electric street lamps ("the lights are visible by mariners many miles out at sea") and its up-to-date system of street railways ("the cables all make a speed of 8½ miles per hour, and the horse lines 7½ miles per hour").

"The little, overgrown town of ten years ago has rapidly developed into a metropolitan city of 40,000 inhabitants," the *Times* reported in the spring of 1886, and when the bubble burst two years later, the Colonel was not disheartened. "The strong currents of the tide of empire," he remained convinced, still ran in the direction of Southern California. From his office in the new Times-Mirror building on the northeast corner of First and Fort Street (Broadway), he looked out over a land that was "waiting for great things—a land where the strength of beauty and glory of civilization may culminate."

The city now extended three miles, instead of two and a half, in each direction from the Plaza. East Los Angeles had become "one of the most beautiful residence sections" and Boyle Heights was "rapidly settling up." At the height of the great boom there had not been a foot of paved street in the city. When Angelinos took inventory on New Year's Day, 1891, they counted 87 miles of paved streets and 78 miles of cement sidewalks. A modern city had sprung up in the last decade, and with its fivefold increase in population (up from 11,311 to 50,394) had come congestion and pollution.

Park commissioners were frantically looking about for open space. "There has, until recently, been so much open ground in all directions within half a mile of the city center that the need of breathing places has not been felt," the *Times* pointed out. Growth had also given rise to fears for the environment. The city engineer was under pressure to devise an effective sewerage system to replace the controversial proposal to carry the main outfall from the southeast corner of the city to the sea ("one of the leading objections to the previous plan was the anticipated pollution of the ocean beach near Santa Monica").

As the 1880s came to an end, however, the *Times* was looking ahead ten years to the dawn of a new century, when "Los Angeles to the ocean will be, not a city, but a succession of beautiful villa homes, each surrounded by from five to twenty acres of productive land." By then, the city's population would have reached 100,000 "and many oldtimers will be telling of the big bargains in real estate which they might have picked up in 1890."

* * *

During the 1890s Angelinos got their first look at horseless carriages, read a prediction that someday the human voice would be transmitted to other planets, listened to warnings from the newly formed Sierra Club ("If we denude our forests, there will be trouble ahead for us"), trooped into Athletic Park to watch the Boston Bloomer Girls play baseball (the home team was made up of theater employees) and clapped a half-hour parking limit on horses hitched in the downtown area.

The completion of the $70,000 Hellman Building at Second and Broadway in 1897 would "contribute to the retention of the business center where it now is, retarding the southerly march of business houses," the *Times* announced, standing bravely against the tide sweeping the city south. Business had been moving in that direction for two generations, ever since John Temple opened his store on the street that bears his name.

The city had been given another southerly shove in the 1880s when Remi Nadeau chose the First and Spring Streets corner now occupied by the *Times* as the site for a grand hotel. It was the first four-story building to pierce the downtown skyline and the first to boast a passenger elevator. The action shifted from the Nadeau to the Van Nuys when it opened its doors at Fourth and Main in January, 1897.

"A neat device for the electrical heating of curling irons in each room is a new feature of special interest to ladies," the *Times* reported.

Eastern travel agents were vying with one another for the most seductive package deal on Southern California excursions. One outfit built a grand hotel in Pasadena and offered its patrons the convenience of traveling "from Boston to the hotel elevator without change of car, and with coupons to pay all their expenses *en route*." A competitor advertised personally conducted tours for sybarites who would not only enjoy the comforts of three drawing room-sleeping cars, but also "a barber shop, bath rooms for ladies and gentlemen, library, grand piano, a stenographer and typewriter, a chaperone and ladies' maid."

Los Angeles, visitors learned from Karl Baedeker's 1893 guidebook to the United States, was founded by the Spaniards in 1781, but was of "no great importance till the ninth decade of the present century, when it underwent an almost unprecedently rapid increase in wealth and population." Its adobe houses, Baedeker pointed out, "have given place almost entirely to stone and brick business blocks and tasteful wooden residences."

The new Angelinos were sweeping aside much of the city's cultural heritage. Streets were named now for Yankee subdividers rather than for Spanish explorers or Mexican colonists. Most of the old names had been obliterated by 1897 when a citizen's committee was appointed to systematize the city's street names. The committee recommended the use of "many Spanish titles, taking care that they shall be appropriate, musical, not too long, and not easily mispronounced."

The City Council agreed to the recommendations, but they were turned down by the mayor. He was afraid the names might "prove very troublesome to newcomers from the East." Among the offending names he cited were Alcantara, Arapahoe, Cerro Gordo, Cimarron, Juanita and Montecito. The city's history had faded so far from memory that a street named for a Mexican governor, Micheltorena, was thought to honor a forgotten Irishman, one Michael Torrance.

Courtesy Security Pacific Bank

Broadway, near Second, as it appeared about the time a couple of tinkerers put together the city's first horseless carriage.

Chapter 3

Oil and Water
1900-1909

> *"The northern half of California is the seat of a relatively old and stable civilization. It has a tradition of good living. Its principal city, San Francisco, is one of the most charming and romantic of American towns ... In Southern California there is no such charm and no such tradition."*
> —H.L. MENCKEN, 1927

EASTERNERS paying their first visit to the west coast around the turn of the century found themselves exploring two Californias. Although statehood forced them to share a common legislative domicile in Sacramento, they lived apart, one in name only. San Francisco, the liberal, worldly, Catholic, trade unionist capital of the north, went in for fine wines and elegant restaurants. South of the Tehachapi Mountains, conservative, provincial, Protestant, open shop Angelinos made do with meatloaf and buttermilk, secure in the knowledge that temperance and industry would be rewarded with prosperity in this world, salvation in the next.

San Francisco, with its port facilities, railway terminals, banks and factories, seemed obviously destined to be the commercial, financial and industrial capital of the American West until the powerful downtown Angelinos who were looking after the city's best interests and their own as well decided the time had come to see that the pueblo acquired what an otherwise bountiful providence had neglected to supply. They set out to dredge a deepwater harbor and build an aqueduct.

In reshaping Southern California to make up for its natural shortcomings, Harrison Gray Otis and his friends in banking, business and manufacturing were simply starting in where their right-thinking, Republican God had left off. General Otis (he'd risen in rank during the war with Spain) and his associates enjoyed a comfortable working relationship with their maker, the sort of deity a man could safely put up for membership in the California Club. The relationship was reflected in a cable the General sent his staff from Yokohama in December, 1906, when the *Times* was about to celebrate its first twenty-five years of publication.

> HOMEWARD BOUND. GRATEFUL FOR ESCAPE FROM OVERMASTERING DISEASE. CONGRATULATIONS ON OUR ANNIVERSARY. REVIEWING SURPASSING ACHIEVEMENTS AND RICH BLESSINGS IN THE PAST QUARTER CENTURY, I REVERENTLY EXCLAIM: "LORD, GOD OF HOSTS, BE WITH US YET, LEST WE FORGET, LEST WE FORGET."

The harbor project pitted General Otis against Collis P. Huntington, president of the Southern Pacific, in a battle for federal funds. The money should go into harbor improvements at San Pedro, the *Times* insisted. The Octopus, eager to control the city's waterfront traffic (and the city as well, of course), fought for a port at Santa Monica. The San Pedro forces organized what they called the Free Habor League and, with the help of Stephen M. White in the United States Senate, managed to derail the Southern Pacific.

Work on the San Pedro breakwater began April 26, 1899, accompanied by suitable oratory, band music and a barbecue. It was finished in 1910. The task of dredging the inner harbor was well along by the time the Panama Canal opened four years later. San Diego and San Francisco, with their splendid natural harbors, found themselves sharing the world's maritime commerce with an inland city.

In the meantime, the city fathers had resorted to some artful gerrymandering. First, in 1906, they had annexed a "shoestring strip" which gave the city a corridor from its southern limits to the San Pedro-Wilmington area. Under state law, however, one incorporated city could not annex another, so Angelinos got the law changed to permit "consolidation." In August, 1909, San Pedro and Wilmington agreed to be consolidated, and the pueblo became a seaport.

As the population shot past the 100,000-mark in 1900, the city saw itself hurtling toward the dread day when it would have to increase its supply of water or decrease its supply of settlers. With limitless growth a basic tenet of their booster faith ("Big is Good, Bigger is Better, Biggest is Best"), Angelinos began to cast about for new sources of water. They had enough to slake the thirst of about 250,000 residents. They were then thinking in terms of 2,000,000.

Fred Eaton, an engineer and a former mayor (1898-1900), had explored the possibility of building an aqueduct to tap the melted snow flowing from the eastern slopes of the Sierra Nevada into the Owens River some 250 miles north of Los Angeles. He persuaded William Mulholland, the municipal water department's superintendent and chief engineer, to look into his scheme. Eaton also had the foresight to file a claim in his own name for much of the river's surplus flow and for land which could be used for dams and reservoirs.

After rattling across the path of the proposed aqueduct in a mule-drawn buckboard, Mulholland pronounced the project feasible and put a price tag on it of something in the neighborhood of $24,500,000. In July, 1905, General Otis sprang it on his readers (TITANIC PROJECT TO GIVE CITY A RIVER). Two months later the city's voters approved a $1,500,000 bond issue to acquire Owens Valley lands and water rights, including the Eaton options. An additional bond issue of $23,000,000 was passed in 1907 and work began on what the press called "The Panama Canal of the West."

No American city had ever faced such an engineering challenge. The 233-mile aqueduct had to pass over foothills, through mountains (its 142 separate tunnels totalled 52 miles) and across the Mojave Desert. But before Mulholland's 5,000-man army could lay a foot of conduit, a 120-mile railroad had to be built to carry heavy machinery into the northern wilderness. Construction crews could be supplied only by building 500 miles of highway and trails which were buried at times by blizzards and sandstorms. Finally, on November 5, 1913, some 40,000 Angelinos turned out to watch the Owens River water cascade into a San Fernando Valley reservoir.

"There it is," said Mulholland, "take it."

Two groups of land speculators were also waiting to take it. The San Fernando Mission Land Company had picked up 16,000 acres of valley land in 1904 with a view to making a profit if and when Henry E. Huntington* ran trolley tracks out from the city. The other syndicate, the Los Angeles Homes Company, representing the interests of General Otis and his son-in-law, Harry Chandler, had acquired some 47,500 acres in 1909-10, counting on the Owens Valley water to enable them to turn a handsome profit.

The water belonged to the city's taxpayers who had put up the money to fetch it from the Sierra Nevada. Before it could be siphoned off to irrigate the San Fernando Valley holdings of the speculators, the city had to go through the formality of annexation. On May 4, 1915, voters obligingly agreed to cram 168 square miles of farming land into the city's borders.

Sale of water to valley ranchers would lower their taxes, they

* Not to be confused with his Uncle Collis who led and lost the fight against the Free Harbor League.

thought. Instead, their taxes went up to pay for the cost of extending city services to such a vast, sparsely settled territory. The San Fernando Valley annexation (Palms was picked up the same day) boosted the city's total area to 280 square miles, exactly ten times the size of the pueblo's land grant from the King of Spain.

* * *

Something deep in the municipal genes has always stirred uneasily at the sight of undisturbed land. In its infancy, the settlement's survival depended on clearing and cultivating the surrounding wilderness. In later years, the pueblo came to regard a stand of cottonwoods or a chaparral covered hillside as a reproach, like the memory of a childhood scolding for having left food on a plate while less fortunate youngsters were going to bed hungry.

"The cottages which are being erected by Mr. Beaudry along the hillside of Fort Street are certainly a very great improvement in that part of town," the *Star* reported in 1870, nearly twenty years before Yankee boosters changed the street's name to Broadway. "Here was a bare and barren hillside, presenting a very repulsive prospect to the beholder."

The owners of Prudent Beaudry's cottages, the editor was happy to add, would be supplied with "all the requisites of water and gas." In short, by taxing Mr. Beaudry's neighbors to pay for the municipal services to be provided purchasers of his viewsite homes, the city had started subsidizing the mutilation of its hills.

"The portion of the city which might be most beautiful and picturesque—all that northern section with its chain of rolling hills—is being utterly ruined through the mistaken greed and ignorance of real estate speculators," the Municipal Art Commission reported in 1909. "With the exception of a very few tracts, on which are laid out beautiful and winding roads that follow the contour, there is a ruthless slashing into hillsides . . . ."

In City Hall, where councilmen were chosen, the *Star* observed in 1860, "from 'good fellows' and 'best citizens,'" it was an article of

Courtesy Security Pacific Bank

Double-parking, a Spring Street nuisance at the turn of the century.

faith that raw land should be taken away from the mule deer and turned over to men of their sort who could be counted to do something with it. Mr. Beaudry was one of the "good fellows" and "best citizens" who dutifully took his turn serving as a city councilman and as mayor.

In their eagerness to dispose of the four square leagues of pueblo lands handed down from the Spaniards, the American city fathers gave away thirty-five-acre "donation lots" in the 1850s to anyone who would spend $200 on improvements within a twelve-month period. Inevitably, the gifts had come back to haunt City Hall in the form of petitions for schools, streets, sewers, water and lights, along with demands for the protective services of the police and fire departments.

"There yet remain a few acres of domain to the city out of tens of thousands, her original heritage," the Mayor reported to the Council as the 1860s drew to a close. "Protect this by every advisable barrier, keep it out of the grasp of the grabber, sharper and speculator."

But the city ran through its royal patrimony like a wastrel prince, flinging away its grandchildren's parks and playgrounds so recklessly that by 1891 the 450 acres of Elysian Park accounted for four-fifths of all the land in the municipal park system. The city fathers had managed to hold onto this last sizeable remnant of their 17,172-acre legacy only because of their inability to give it away, much less sell it.

* * *

Henry E. Huntington left San Francisco in 1902 and moved to Los Angeles, determined to "join this whole region in one big family." A generation of Angelinos rode his red (interurban) and yellow (local) trolley cars to the office, the theater, the beach and the mountains. Racing along at speeds of forty and fifty miles an hour (the horse car had moved at the rate of seven and one-half miles an hour), the Pacific Electric cars enabled Southern Californians to live among orange trees and work in downtown skyscrapers.

"Los Angeles is a busy centre for short trips, chiefly made now by electric cars," *Baedeker's United States* informed travelers in 1909.

The local fare was five cents. It cost fifteen cents to make the half-hour trip to Pasadena ("a thriving business city and health resort"). The hour-long, fifty-cent journey to Santa Monica took tourists through Hollywood ("a suburb of charming homes"), and could be extended to Venice ("with canals, etc., in imitation of its European namesake"). For a dollar, the big spenders could travel a hundred miles along the Pacific Electric's "Great Surf Route," which included not only Long Beach ("a frequented summer resort, with 2,250 inhab.") and San Pedro ("the National Government is now constructing a huge breakwater here"), but also Compton ("the centre of the dairy district").

In the first decade of the new century, as Pacific Electric tracks snaked across the countryside, the population of Los Angeles tripled (from 102,479 to 319,198). Long Beach shot up from 2,252 to 17,809, Santa Monica from 3,057 to 7,847, Redondo Beach from 855 to 2,935 and Burbank from 3,048 to 12,255.

"City making now is different from that of previous times," the editor of the *Express* pointed out on a fall day in 1905, shortly after Angelinos had agreed to go along with the acquisition of Owens Valley water rights. "Modern transportation methods make it possible to weave into a harmonious unit a larger section than was possible until late years."

Even if Greater Los Angeles stretched out twenty-five miles to both the northwest and the southeast, as seemed probable, a commuter would still be able to pick a fresh boutonniere from his garden, catch an interurban electric car and reach his downtown office within an hour. Warming to the message of his tea leaves, the editor went on to describe a future city which would serve as "the world's symbol of all that is beautiful and healthful and inspiring."

"It will retain the flowers and orchards and lawns, the invigorating free air from the ocean, the bright sunshine and the elbow room, which have marked it as peculiar in the past and which now are secured for all time by the abundance of the water supply. It will not become congested like the older cities, for the transportation lines, built in advance of the demands, have made it possible to get far out in the midst of the orchards and fields for home making."

The pattern for the city's sprawling development had been established by the world's finest mass rapid transit system. No one foresaw its doom when, at two o'clock on a May morning in 1897, a pair of tinkerers rolled a four-cylinder horseless carriage out of a West Fifth Street shop and took a few friends on a trial spin through the business district.

"One fear which had been felt beforehand was that the machine would scare horses, because of its unique appearance and because of the noise of the gasoline motors and the gasoline explosions," the *Times* reported. "A number of teams were passed during the trial trip, but they showed not the slightest fear of the novel spectacle."

* * *

At the time the city's first gasoline-powered tallyho rattled past mule teams on Main Street, some 500 hundred wells were pumping oil in an area roughly bounded by Figueroa, First, Union and Temple. The oil boom had been launched by Edward L. Doheny in November, 1892, with a well dug near the present intersection of Second Street and Glendale Boulevard.

"This is one of the leading industries of the city, and all legislation bearing on it should be liberal," warned the incoming mayor in January, 1897, when the City Council was working on an ordinance forbidding drilling operations near city parks.

Angelinos, caught up in the Black Gold Rush of the 1890s were living above a supply so abundant that, as the *News* had pointed out in 1865, "whole tracts of land are found in this region which cannot be traversed on foot, in consequence of the thick coating of soft 'tar.'" The tar, or *brea* as the oldtimers called it, was congealed petroleum.

Courtesy Security Pacific Bank

A massive display of force by the city's mounted constabulary in the early years of the new century.

The Indians had used it to caulk their boats and waterproof their woven baskets. The *gente de razon* had covered their roofs with it to ward off the winter rains. It was still keeping Angelinos dry on January 24, 1865 when a group of their wealthy neighbors got together and formed the Pioneer Oil Company "for the purpose of prospecting for petroleum." It was to be used to light lamps and grease axles. Three weeks later the editor of the *News* drove out to the "city *brea* lands" to look in on the wildcatters.

"It will be no small astonishment to our citizens to find that incalculable fortunes lie in the very substance with which, as many of them believe, they have been 'sorely afflicted'; that which they have 'scraped from their shoes' for three-quarters of a century past," the editor wrote, and one Saturday evening the following March he conducted an experiment.

He stopped by the Main Street "oil headquarters" of Sackett & Morgan and bought four ounces of locally produced coal oil (or "kerosine," as some called it). He poured the sample into one of the lamps used for setting type and filled another lamp with eastern coal oil. The local product ignited more readily, burned more brightly ("without the slightest wavering") and left no crust on the wick.

"We can produce an article of oil in abundance, which is equal, if not vastly superior to anything of the kind now held in the market," the editor declared, and before autumn had run its course guests at the Bella Union Hotel were dining by the light of "a fine quality of refined coal oil" from a San Fernando Valley refinery.

The California product, however, failed to live up to the hopes of its backers or the testimonial of the *News* editor. Refiners didn't know how to cope with raw material which contained less paraffin and more carbon than eastern crude oil. As a result, the lubricating oils were more watery than those from back East, and the kerosine more likely to blacken lamp chimneys with smoke. Even worse, the local oils were usually more expensive. Some seventy oil companies sprang up during California's shortlived boom.

When it collapsed in 1867, all save one went under.

"The employment of petroleum, and the various preparations made from it, is becoming very general throughout the world, superseding candles, whale, palm, and other oils for illuminating as well as lubricating purposes and generating steam," the *Daily News* editorialized in the spring of 1872, and the following June the *Star* insisted that unless "our entire population are fools," Angelinos should establish an oil refinery and get on with the business of "developing our oil region into one of the most extensive and valuable properties in the United States."

In the 1890s, when California ranked as the country's third oil-producing state (behind Pennsylvania and New York), Los Angeles emerged as the oil capital of the West. Wildcatters watched the price of crude shoot up from $1.20 to $1.80 a barrel in 1900, and a few years later sink to fifteen cents. The automobile, with its insatiable thirst for petroleum products, was still a rich man's plaything.

Natural gas usually shows up wherever crude oil is found, and back in the 1870s an enterprising outfit had peddled illuminating gas from Ventura County to northern Californians with the sales pitch that it was "superior to coal gas in light and purity, and moves through the meters less swiftly," but for years California oil companies continued to rid themselves of the nuisance by burning it in the field.

Oil and gas came to mind when William Andrew Spalding, reminiscing about the city's mood at the turn of the century, commented on the unfailing cheerfulness of Angelinos in the face of adversity. They had seen their cattle die, their banks fail and their real estate boom collapse; they had survived earthquakes, fires, floods and the Southern Pacific, and always they had "come up smiling after each throw-down" and gone on with the business of building a metropolis.

"When an oil belt was developed within the city boundaries which seemed to bring as much destruction of values as it produced—when there was no system, no order—when oil went to waste and the gas escaped—when there was no market for the product, and the price fell to ten cents a barrel—then the people addressed themselves to solving the strange problem, this embarrassment of riches.

"They constructed storage tanks, and devised means of transportation; they invented burners, and learned how to use the crude oil for steam generation and brick-making; they learned how to utilize the crude oil in road making; they acquired the art and devised the apparatus for refining; they discovered a way for saving and utilizing the gas that had been escaping from their wells; they prospected with 'wild-cat' boring until they had extended the territory miles outside of the originally developed area. In short, they established one of the greatest petroleum fields in the world. With such a record of courage, persistence and achievement, it is no wonder that Los Angeles began the new century with a stout heart and a confident air."

* * *

January 1, 1900, marked the start of the last year of the nineteenth century, but in Los Angeles, as in many other parts of the world, it was celebrated as the beginning of a new century. Fifty thousand spectators showed up for Pasadena's eleventh annual Tournament of Roses. "Every train and every electric car was crammed," the *Times* reported, and noted that every available tallyho, coach and rig within a twenty-mile radius of Orange Grove Boulevard was also pressed into service. While waiting for the parade to pass by, Angelinos read about the Boers in South Africa (they were losing their war) and the Americans in the Philippines (they were winning).

A 1900 Yale Bicycle was available for $35 ("We sell on installments") and, for $5, "a full set of teeth on rubber." Hypochondriacs could load up on cod liver oil ("the standard remedy for lung trouble") and, depending on sex, Ajax tablets ("Made Me a Man") or French Female Pills. They could also apply to an

Courtesy Security Pacific Bank

One of the Victorian showplaces of the prospering city.

Oriental Seer who was prepared to give "valuable advice concerning all matters of health, obscure or nervous disease, evil habits and weaknesses of men and women." If all else failed, a bottle of eight-year-old Plantation Whiskey could be had for seventy-five cents.

The Mayor was concerned about the size of the police force ("totally inadequate") and the City Council with its refusal to enforce a new ordinance regulating the height of billboards. "If the chair had the authority," declared the council president, "he would take every officer on the police force and chop down all the billboards in the city." H. Gaylord Wilshire, a flamboyant Socialist who enjoyed a monopoly on billboards at the time, countered with the remark that they "soothed and satisfied the esthetic sense."

Visually, the city was suffering the modern blight of billboards, light standards and power lines, but morally it had undergone a reformation at the hands of the white Anglo-Saxon Protestants who had defected during the boom years from county seat law offices, drug stores, dairy barns, funeral parlors and Baptist parsonages. They had proceeded to rip the vine leaves from the pueblo's hair and turn a Latin carnival into a midwestern covered-dish supper. In their efforts to keep their neighbors from pleasuring themselves, especially on Sunday, they made life miserable for the three councilmen who, in the late 1890s served on the City Council's Committee on Public Morals.

The committee was badgered with demands for ordinances restraining hotels and restaurants from selling cigars on Sunday and prohibiting anyone under the age of fifteen from being "on the streets, alleys or public places of the City of Los Angeles at night after nine o'clock." They sought to outlaw "the exhibition of photographic or kinetoscopic pictures representing prize fights" and when the city's Yankee traders and moneylenders announced plans for an old fashioned fiesta, the reformers scurried down to City Hall to plump for an ordinance forbidding the wearing of masks "on the streets from sunset until sunrise during La Fiesta."

The Committee on Public Morals managed to keep a straight face when it reported to the council on a summer day in 1897: "Whereas, the morals of the City of the Angels have reached as near perfection as may be expected, we therefore see no further use for this committee, and recommend that this committee be discharged and stricken from the list of standing committees of this council." The recommendation was adopted.

* * *

Angelinos in 1909 were talking about downtown traffic jams, the need for a central library, a new ordinance shunting smokers to the back of streetcars, the search for a humane way of disposing of stray dogs, the tenfold increase in the cost of collecting garbage during the year, a Packard dealer's proposal to connect Los Angeles and San Francisco with an automobile highway, and the soaring salaries of city employees, some of whom were knocking down $300 a month.

"Like a profligate son, Los Angeles is spending its great income from taxation on office holders, and is saving for permanent improvements but a mere shred of the millions that are poured into the treasury annually," the *Times* declared, and proceeded to plump for a Union Station and a new city hall which, the editors hoped, would help anchor property on Spring Street against the city's commercial drift down Broadway.

City fathers had taken a chance in transferring the thirty-seven-year-old public library to a department store "somewhat outside what was last year deemed 'the business center,'" the library's board of commissioners reported. Now, however, the shoppers flocking to Hamburger's Eighth and Broadway emporium were dropping by the third floor to pick up or return a book (Elinor Glyn was the contemporary Harold Robbins).

When the city's second annual automobile show opened in Hamburger's basement in late January, Angelinos boasted of having more cars per capita on their streets than any other city in the world and enthusiasts foresaw the day when "auto trucks will successfully compete with the steam roads" in moving goods from San Pedro to Los Angeles. While Don Lee's Cadillac 30 was racking up local sales records, other dealers were pushing the new Pope-Hartford, Reo, Peerless, Auburn ("equipped with gas tank") and "that foreign looking car," the Oldsmobile ("note the Mercedes type radiator").

Los Angeles, the first city to come up with a procedure for recalling its elected officials, decided to put the novel procedure in operation in February, when petitions were circulated for the ousting of Mayor Arthur C. Harper, who was charged with involvement in gambling and prostitution.

"I was raised in a Christian home," he said in denying the charges, but six weeks later he resigned.

Although there was now no mayor to recall, the city attorney insisted the election must proceed as ordered by its petitioners. Voters were given a choice between Fred Wheeler, a Socialist, and George Alexander, a seventy-year-old Iowa defector backed by the Good Government Organization. Alexander won and took the oath of office on April Fool's Day.

"The time is not far distant," he said a few months later, "when our cherished dream of one great and beautiful city 'from the mountains to the sea' will be realized."

Local realtors were touting Mount Washington lots ("the grandest residential viewpoint available to homeseekers in Southern California") for their unique offering of "a real mountain, with real mountain views, all within twenty minutes of the skyscrapers of Broadway." Out west, Laurel Canyon had opened the door on Lookout Mountain Park, designed "for the busy and ever growing population of Los Angeles and Hollywood to get out and up into the restful, charming mountains."

While the city and county were working out an agreement to come up with $250,000 for a museum in Agricultural Park, a science teacher at Los Angeles High School got permission to take his students out to Rancho La Brea ("six miles west of Los

Angeles," a newspaper report explained), where they dug up some bones of the extinct creatures that prowled Southern California in the Pleistocene Age.

"The women have just begun to fight," Mrs. Lillian Harris of San Francisco assured her militant sisters in Los Angeles when the state assembly turned down a proposed constitutional amendment giving women the vote. When a woman active in the work of the Humane Animal League was appointed "poundmistress," she was unable to take the job because the city's charter restricted it to "qualified electors," a specification only enfranchised males could meet.

By the end of the year the city had acquired the land it wanted for a civic center and French fliers were steaming across the Atlantic with their crated planes to take part in the country's first international air meet, to be staged by the Aero Club of Southern California at Dominguez Field. Two local automobile dealers were preparing to offer planes for sale and the *Times* was predicting that with in a few years "the aeroplane will be as popular in Southern California as the automobile is today."

In a couple of weeks, with the setting of two world records in the skies of Southern California (an altitude of 4,165 feet and a speed of fifty-five miles per hour for a plane carrying a passenger), an awed journalist would suggest that airships might someday have to be used for warlike purposes "just once in order to teach the world the most terrible lesson in its history." It was a sobering start for the new year.

Main Street looking north, 1907.

Chapter 4

Stars Over Otistown
1910-1919

> *"On Wednesday, January 19, the entire Biograph stock company with Lawrence Griffith, director-in-chief, was dispatched on fast trains to the sunny and picturesque land of Southern California."*
>
> —THE MOVING PICTURE WORLD,
> January 29, 1910

ALTHOUGH his name was unfamiliar to the editors of *The Moving Picture World*, David Wark Griffith had ground out 142 films for Biograph the year before he talked the company into letting him winter in Southern California with his cameraman (Billy Bitzer) and a covey of photoplayers (Mack Sennett and sixteen-year-old Mary Pickford, among others). On the third day of his trip west, Griffith turned thirty-five. The following Sunday he debarked at Los Angeles, where Selig Polyscope and the New York Motion

Picture Company had already set up shop.

"Most of the moving pictures made in America are produced in Los Angeles," the *Times* reported February 1, while Griffith was renting a vacant lot next door to a lumberyard at the corner of Grand Avenue and Washington Street.

"Our studio," Mary Pickford recalled years later in her autobiography, "consisted of an acre of ground, fenced in, and a large wooden platform, hung with cotton sheets that were pulled on wires overhead. On a windy day our clothes and curtains on the set would flap loudly in the breeze. Studios were all on open lots—roofless and without walls, which explains the origin of the term, 'on the lot.'"

Biograph was one of the major film-producers that had banded together in 1908 to freeze out competition by forming the Motion Picture Patents Company. William Selig, a colorful Chicago maverick, whose one-reel version of *The Count of Monte Cristo*, had been filmed in Los Angeles, responded by sending Francis Boggs, a writer-director, and Thomas Parsons, a cameraman-business manager, back to Southern California with a view to making pictures in sun-drenched surroundings far removed from patent lawyers, process servers and hired thugs.

"We have tried every part of the world and we find that Los Angeles is the best place to make our pictures," Boggs said in 1909, when he started shooting his westerns in the badlands of Edendale, north of Alvarado and Sunset.

At the time Griffith turned up in Los Angeles some two hundred picture players were working in films which cost from $500 to $3,000, often required an entire week to make and could be seen in fourteen minutes. The moviemakers had come at first to escape snow and ice, the *Times* reported, "but the bright quality of the sunshine and the number of clear days in which they may work, together with the variety of scenery, has all been found ideal." The upstart industry, the paper was convinced, had come to stay.

An estimated 4,000,000 men, women and children were daily customers of the country's 10,000 to 12,000 motion picture houses and in Los Angeles, a local exhibitor told the *Times*, several families "now own their picture machines, just as they do their phonograph, and come in regularly to rent films." But despite the popularity of the world's new toy, the men and women who appeared before the cameras were as little known as the directors. The licensed companies insisted on preserving the anonymity of their actors in order to hold down salaries.

"The interest the public has taken in the personality of the picture players is astonishing," *The Moving Picture World* reported, May 14, 1910, the issue which carried a review of *Ramona*, the most ambitious of Griffith's first batch of California films. The reviewer did not identify "the Biograph artist" responsible for the picture's "splendid" artistic quality and none of the cast (Mary Pickford played an Indian girl) was named. Before the year was out, however, the editors saw fit to devote a full page to Miss Pickford, "an artiste of the highest rank in a field where there are very few of her kind."

After neglecting Southern California filmmaking news for ten months, the trade publication reprinted a long *Los Angeles Times* article in which local theatrical men predicted, "Los Angeles will be the moving picture center of America next year." To underscore the city's growing importance to distributors and exhibitors in Chicago, New York, and Philadelphia, the editors inaugurated a column, "Notes from the Coast Studios." Selig's new glass-and-steel studio, the columnist reported, had solar heat. "The refraction of the sunlight through the glass heats the studio like a battery of steam operators."

* * *

Along with its "splendid material assets," General Otis noted with satisfaction in January, 1910, Los Angeles enjoyed "that priceless boon, industrial freedom." His nearly thirty years of anti-union crusading in the *Times* had made "Otistown," as labor leaders called it, the country's most impregnable open shop fortress. In recent months, however, the city's General Labor Council had managed to unite warring factions within the labor movement and the local economy's continuing shift from farms to factories was changing the industrial relations climate.

Meanwhile in San Francisco, where employers had long complained of Southern California's open shop competition, union strategists had decided it was high time they set out to equalize wages and working conditions on both sides of the Tehachapis. Organizers zeroed in on the metal trades workers, hoping not only to improve the lot of their laboring brothers in Los Angeles but also to protect the closed shop benefits of their Bay Area members.

In mid-July, six weeks after the metal trades unions ordered a walkout, the City Council unanimously adopted a stiff antipicketing ordinance that carried a fine of $100 and a jail term of up to fifty days. By the end of September the strike had cost the labor movement more than $80,000 in bail, fines, benefits and lawyers' fees, but in those first nine months of the year the Central Labor Council had grown from sixty-two unions with 6,000 members to eighty-five unions with approximately 9,500 members.

When the city's trade unionists went to bed on Friday night, September 30, they had cause to sleep well. Never had they been more confident of their ability to storm Otistown and organize its workers. Then, at 1:07 A.M., they were awakened by an explosive rumbling many of them took to be an earthquake and when they joined the crowd swarming around First and Broadway, they saw their hopes for organization go up in the flames that gutted the *Times* building.

"I stood across the street watching the smoking ruins," Will Robinson wrote nearly sixty years later. "I had hurried to the scene from my boarding house near USC, where I was a freshman student, having heard an early morning rumor of the tragedy. I looked at the smoldering heap from which none of the dead had yet been removed. Over it the smoke rose like a murky and acrid fog. Pushing through the crowd I was able to buy a copy of the four-page edition of the *Times* which had been rushed out—an almost unbelievable achievement—at an auxiliary plant."

The headline screamed organized labor's responsibility for the assault that had killed twenty employees: UNIONIST BOMB WRECKS THE TIMES. Otis, on his way back to Los Angeles from Mexico, arrived that afternoon and found a time-bomb planted at his home. Police got it outside before it exploded. A similar "infernal device" turned up at the home of the secretary of the Merchants' and Manufacturers' Association. It proved to be a dud.

"The purpose of the crime was not merely to destroy the plant of the *Times* and kill and maim the men who were in the building, but to break, if possible, its contact with the great free and independent mass of citizens of Los Angeles and Southern California, who have refused to bow the knee to labor union dictation," the *Times* declared, and an editorial bearing the General's stamp warned "the devils in human form" who had done this deed that "ropes are dangling for them."

Organized labor was unanimous in its protestations of innocence and in its expression of sympathy for the victims and their families. Most trade unionists thought the disaster was an accident, the result of a gas leak, but some extremists went so far as to implicate Otis himself in what he called "the crime of the century."

"Since 1901," Grace Stimson points out in *Rise of the Labor Movement in Los Angeles*, "he had made no substantial improvements in the old building, evidently a fire trap with a faulty gas system, but instead had drawn up complete plans for a new structure. Furthermore, Otis had built and fully equipped an auxiliary plant for any emergency. Even more curious, according to an investigatory committee of the California State Federation of Labor, was the fact that despite the quickness of the flames the *Times* had lost no valuable records and no executive personnel in the conflagration."

Many of those who tacitly accepted labor's guilt felt that Otis bore part of the blame. For years, as the *Pacific Outlook* reminded its readers, he had thrown kerosene on the flames of local labor disputes. Frederick Palmer, writing for *Hampton's Magazine*, reported: "You hear talk of the hateful baiting which breeds hate; of a man of power and position using his newspaper weapon with such venom in beating down his enemies that he created the elements which could find no voice except nitroglycerin to answer the dynamite of Otis' language."

Samuel Gompers, president of the American Federation of Labor, was confident of the innocence of union members. "The greatest enemies of our movement," he told a Michigan audience, "could not administer a blow so hurtful to our cause as would be such a stigma if the men of organized labor were responsible for it."

Mayor Alexander called in William J. Burns, a detective known for his services to bankers, merchants and manufacturers. His investigation of similar bombings of nonunion plants led him to the Indianapolis headquarters of the International Association of Bridge and Structural Iron Workers, a young organization which, in the last five years, had exploded eighty-seven bombs around the country. Burns persuaded Ortie McManigal, a member of the union, to sign a sworn statement incriminating both John J. McNamara, the union's secretary-treasurer, and his brother, James. It was James who, according to Burns' evidence, had actually planted the bomb at the *Times*.

The brothers were arrested and brought to Los Angeles in April, 1911. The American Federation of Labor, suspicious of McManigal's confession and outraged by Burns' highhanded method of spiriting John McNamara out of his home state, launched a nationwide campaign for a defense fund. Gompers personally talked a reluctant Clarence Darrow into taking their case. He arrived in Los Angeles in May and several weeks later, on July 12, they pleaded not guilty to the charges in the indictments against them. In September, during a west coast tour to drum up support for the brothers, Gompers visited them in jail and was assured of their innocence.

Darrow's defense team included not only a brace of respectable local attorneys with access to Otis and his peers in the downtown establishment, but also Job Harriman, the Socialist lawyer who had spearheaded labor's attack on the city's antipicketing law. When Harriman ran for mayor that fall, the returns from the October 31 primary chilled capitalist spines. He came out ahead of George Alexander, the grandfatherly incumbent placed in City Hall by municipal reformers. The runoff election was set for December 5.

On Tuesday, November 28, voters on both sides were shocked to learn that Bert Franklin, Darrow's chief investigator, had been arrested for bribing a prospective juror to hold out for James McNamara's acquittal. When the trial resumed the following Friday morning, December 1, after a Thanksgiving Day recess, the district attorney was given an adjournment of a few hours to consider "grave matters." That afternoon the McNamara brothers came before the presiding judge and sent reporters scurrying toward every available telephone by changing their pleas to guilty.

"They had it on us," Darrow said. "The county had a complete case. There was no loophole."

"God's people spoke," the *Times* announced next day, "and the enemies of God stand confused. Scoffing, anarchistic Socialism has been crushed—as far as this city is concerned—with the same swift merciless annihilation that the heel of a giant crushed the head of a reptile..."

While voters were going to the polls (women were casting their ballots in a city election for the first time), the McNamara brothers were brought into court to hear their sentences pronounced. James McNamara, in a brief written statement, told of placing sixteen sticks of dynamite in Ink Alley, the passageway between the *Times* and stereotyping and press rooms, at 5:45 P.M., September 30. The time-bomb triggered a second and even more devastating explosion of tons of inflammable ink, which spread flames through the old building so quickly that rescuers were unable to reach the men trapped inside.

"It was my intention to injure the building and scare the

owners," McNamara stated in his confession. "I did not intend to take the life of anyone. I sincerely regret these unfortunate men lost their lives."

He was given life imprisonment, his brother got fifteen years.

"For socialism and for organized labor it was a most bitter blow," John Caughey writes. "Instead of being swept into office as he confidently expected, Job Harriman was hopelessly snowed under in the Los Angeles election. Socialist candidates elsewhere were adversely affected, and the Socialist party never regained the strength or promise that it enjoyed prior to the McNamara confession. For the next twenty or twenty-five years the same can almost be said of the American Federation of Labor."

* * *

"Locally, the motion picture people may be something of a pest, but their value to the community as national and international advertisers is inestimable," the *Times* observed in its first editorial on the film industry, January 17, 1911.

Within a year five large companies (Biograph, Selig, Pathé, Kalem and Bison) were at work in Los Angeles, along "with a host of smaller fry." The city had become a backdrop for films "exhibited all over the civilized world, the daily audience of the licensed manufacturers alone being computed at 20,000,000, while the 'independents' show to millions more." The motion picture had proved to be so powerful in "advertising Americanism outside of American boundaries" that Britons were reported to be "tremendously stirred up over what is termed the Americanization of Canada by American filmmakers."

A feature writer, taking note of the tourists gawking at studio gates as they passed through Edendale on their way to "one of the famous Spanish dinners of Glendale," described the sort of "remarkable antics" he had stumbled on in covering the film factories:

"A lovely young lady in her nightdress, an emigrant woman with a child (dummy) in her arms, the captain of a steamship and two officers, several barefooted, ragged sailors, a couple of gentlemen who had evidently dressed in a hurry and had only blankets over their shoulders, a young hero in open-neck shirt, and a droll-looking little fat man with old fashioned plug hat and carpet bag in one hand, all prancing around on the grass while the Jap gardener turned the hose on them. The women were screaming shrilly as the cold water ran down their necks, and the men danced, Indian-like, with a look of sullen suffering on their faces, while the Jap boy grinned delightfully at the fun of 'soaking it to 'em.' The explanation of it all was that the players were about to go into the studio in a shipwreck scene."

Edendale, where the first filmmakers clustered their studios, lay between Los Angeles and Hollywood, a pleasant suburb, with a population of about 5,000. Laid out in 1883 by a Kansas Prohibitionist, H. H. Wilcox, it had been incorporated in 1903 and described two years later as a sober, God-fearing place "where the saloon and its kindred evils are unknown." It was gobbled up by Los Angeles in 1910, when the prospect of sharing the city's Owens Valley water made annexation an attractive and profitable option for neighboring communities.

In the early fall of that same year David Horsley, president of a Staten Island film company, turned up in Los Angeles looking for a place to make movies. He took over an abandoned roadhouse on the northwest corner of Sunset Boulevard and Gower Street, and turned it into Hollywood's first motion picture studio. Not until three years later did the *Times* first mention Hollywood in connection with the making of motion pictures.

"The new stage of the Universal studios at Hollywood is fully occupied continually and holds three sets at one time," the paper reported, February 20, 1913.

In that same year Cecil B. DeMille, who had played Mary Pickford's brother in her first Broadway play, rented a Vine Street barn in Hollywood and started shooting a feature film, *The Squaw Man*, starring a high-priced ($5,000) Broadway star, Dustin Farnum. DeMille had offered his older brother, William, a chance to come in with him and his two partners in forming the Jesse L. Lasky Feature Play Company, but William, a successful playwright (he'd written the play in which his brother and Mary Pickford had been given small parts), refused to have anything to do with the making of these overgrown peepshows. Four years later he could have sold his $5,000 quarter-interest in the company for more than $2 million.

William DeMille was in the Longacre Theater audience gathered in the late spring of 1914 for the first showing of his brother's film. Never having seen a motion picture that told a full-length, dramatic story, his expectations were modest. He attended out of a sense of family loyalty, mulling over the expressions of "affectionate sympathy" he expected to offer C.B. when the ordeal was over.

"The house darkened and the picture began to appear," he wrote in *Hollywood Saga*. "Much to my amazement, I found myself first interested, then held and finally moved by it."

When tears came to his eyes and a catch to his throat, when he saw that everyone else in the theater had also been brought under the picture's spell, he realized something important was taking place. "I had my first vision of what this new art was bound to become," he wrote; "how it was, inevitably, to serve untold millions of people. In spite of its obvious faults, limitations and silence, I saw unrolled before my eyes the first really new form of dramatic story-telling which had been invented for some 500 years."

By 1917 the manufacture of motion pictures had become the country's fifth largest industry and, the *Times* noted, "some rate it as high as third or fourth." Would-be cinema monopolists, in the meantime, had been done in not only by the courts but also by their own greed and short-sightedness in refusing to publicize their picture players and in stubbornly sticking to their one-reelers at a time when Americans were devouring their first fan magazines and standing in line to see *The Birth of a Nation.*

* * *

Willard Huntington Wright, who surfaced from a sickbed in the 1920s as the popular mystery writer, S. S. Van Dine, was graduated from Santa Monica High School, where he set a record for the 100-yard dash, and from St. Vincent's College, where classmates later remembered him for his modish wardrobe and his dazzling performance on the diamond and the gridiron. He did some graduate work at Harvard and in 1910 went to work for the *Los Angeles Times* as its literary editor. Three years later, *Smart Set* published his classic putdown of Los Angeles.

The city had grown too rapidly, Wright felt. Its population had reached nearly half a million, but temperamentally it was still an overgrown village, with "memories of the milk can, the newmown hay, the Chautauqua lecturers, the plush albums, the hamlet devotions and the weekly baths." The new breed of Angelino had come from the Middle West with "a complete stock of rural beliefs, pieties, superstitions and habits," along with "a righteous abhorrence of shapely legs" and "an aversion to late dinners, malt liquors, grand opera and hussies."

Wright gave the back of his hand to the city's restaurants ("little more than magnified village lunch rooms"), its lack of nighttime diversions ("the city's lights go out at twelve, and so does the drummer's hopes"), its cultural shortcomings ("at concerts they applaud the high notes"), its women ("they vote, storm the curbstone tables to sign petitions of protest") and its eccentrics ("spiritualists, mediums, astrologists, phrenologists, palmists, and all other breeds of esoteric windjammers").

Two generations of East Coast journalists have paid their children's orthodontic bills by improvising variations on the themes

Wright first sounded in *Smart Set* ("You can drink in a drive-in saloon, eat in a cafe shaped like a toad, and when you die, they will bury you in a 'Happy Cemetery,' " chortled the *Saturday Evening Post* in 1945), but few of them seem to have read his final paragraphs.

"The city reeks with promise," he declared, after speaking of the great problems being worked out within its borders. No city was more heterogeneous, he added and proceeded to praise its wit ("not the wit of epigram and culture, but the wit of serious endeavor"). He concluded with a vision of "a metropolis wealthy and diverse, commercially powerful and artistically wise."

Writing in the same year, 1913, Harris Newmark wound up his delightful and indispensable memoirs, *Sixty Years in Southern California*, with a forecast of the not distant day when the city he had first known as a dusty, adobe village diverting its sewage to the wilds of Sixth and Main would be "a world-center prominent in almost every field of human endeavor."

While Wright, the sophisticated critic, and Newmark, the pioneer merchant, were taking different routes across the city's lively past to reach the same conclusion about its future, crystal-ball gazers were looking ahead twenty-five years and giving *Times* readers a glimpse of the city as it might appear in 1938, when Angelinos would be nipping about in aermobiles and living in handsome apartment on Figueroa near Adams Boulevard, a district "sometimes compared to Riverside Drive in New York City."

In the up-to-date homes of 1938, automatic scrubbing machines and electric vacuum cleaners would have "taken much of the manual work out of the hands of maids and oriental help," and each house would have its own refrigerating plant. Thanks to a new thermostat method of ventilation, it would not be necessary "to open a single window throughout the entire year, while still keeping the house freshened with the finest possible air and at a temperature desired."

"All the world joined in the craze to come to Los Angeles and secure a home in some of its environing valleys and mountains," the prophets declared, and projected a population of 1,532,000 by 1930.*

* * *

On the eve of the first world war, *Times*-readers sympathized with Theda Bara ("I cried for two days and lost fourteen pounds over having to appear in a one-piece bathing suit in *A Fool There Was*"), followed the debate over the opening of Arizona's Indian lands ("it is neither wise nor just to withhold the fairest and richest sections of the new state from her citizens"), discussed air pollution ("on a clear day from the top of Mt. Lowe the effect of Los Angeles smoke on the surrounding pellucid air is evident and apparent as a gray-brown veil hanging over the city") and followed the exchanges between their new reform governor, Hiram Johnson, and General Otis (Otis described Johnson as a "bombastic, self-assertive, conceited, dominating man" and the governor pictured the publisher as a man "with a gangrened heart and rotting brain, grimacing at every reform, chattering impotently at all things that are decent").

In the San Fernando Valley, where the general had substantial real estate holdings, the Van Nuys and Lankershim ranches had been transformed from "a vast wheatfield to a thriving center of villages and suburban homes." There was talk in 1912 of a "15-mile speedway" linking Los Angeles with Van Nuys, a town with a bank, a newspaper and a population of 550. When 108,732 acres of the Valley were annexed by Los Angeles in 1915, a lone policeman patrolled what was publicized as the world's largest beat.

General Otis, during the following year, took President Wilson to task for appointing Louis Brandeis to the Supreme Court ("enough to make cold chills run down the spine of every patriot in the country"), rebuked the Friday Morning Club for turning its podium over to the anarchist "prattlings" of Upton Sinclair ("this slim, beflanneled example of perverted masculinity"), joined other local dignitaries on the reviewing stand of the city's Preparedness Day parade and announced his decision to give his

---

* It was 1,238,048 in 1930 and 1,504,277 in 1940.

Wilshire Boulevard mansion, The Bivouac, to the county to serve as a "home for the fine arts."

The eighty-year-old publisher was living in Hollywood with his daughter, Marian, and her husband, Harry Chandler, in late July, 1917 when he expressed a desire one morning to visit his San Fernando Valley Ranch. "Harry, I want you to go with me today instead of my chauffeur," he told his son-in-law, and invited his two grandsons to tag along. Although a recent angina attack had slowed him down a bit, he was in high spirits that day, joking and punning. When he got home that evening, however, he was so weak that for the first time he had to ask for help in walking into the house.

He awoke at 7:30 next morning, July 30, had a cup of coffee and read the Sunday *Times* ("America," Herbert Hoover was quoted in a front-page story, "will win the war"). At 9 o'clock the Chandlers' maid, Lucy, brought his breakfast upstairs on a tray. He picked at his food and then, suddenly clapping a hand over his heart, he said quietly, without excitement, "Take away the tray, Lucy. I'm gone." The Chandlers, downstairs at the breakfast table, heard the maid's screams and ran up to the bedroom. There was no detectable pulse.

"In an intercourse of years," one of his editorial writers pointed out next day, "*Times* writers on all subjects became so saturated with the Otis spirit and the Otis opinions that they seldom misinterpreted him in dealing with the issues of the day."

The dead general spoke through an Otis-saturated writer some months later when the paper needled the International Alliance of Theatrical Stage Employees for trying to enforce a clause demanding that employers agree "not to support or encourage any school for the instruction of women or girls in the operation of motion picture machines, nor employ women or girl machine operators." Trade unionists had always been "the selfish foe of women," the writer declared, and went on to muse, "No wonder there are feminists and suffragettes, no wonder a sex war looms large for the future."

* * *

When the Panama Canal opened August 15, 1914, the steamship *Missourian*, eleven days out of New York, was waiting at Colon. Nine days, twenty hours and forty-five minutes later the captain brought her into the harbor at San Pedro, the first ship to reach Los Angeles by way of the great ditch linking the Atlantic and Pacific oceans. Some 8,000 miles had been lopped from the Argonauts' long, rough voyage around Cape Horn in '49.

"An uneventful trip," the captain reported.

He had left New York on August 4, the day England declared war on Germany. Four years later, in the closing weeks of the war, a truck carrying a three-ton load covered the 3,450 miles between the two coasts in twenty days, promising to "revolutionize anew the history of transportation." While oldtimers taking the sun in Central Park swapped stories of the Southern Pacific's arrogance, a new generation of merchants and manufacturers lifted a noonday glass to the city's deliverance by land and sea from the tyranny of the railroads.

During the war years Angelinos built ships and airplanes, bought Thrift Stamps and Liberty Bonds, registered 4,000 enemy aliens, kept a suspicious eye on Mexico, banned the teaching of German in public schools, cut down on their use of gasoline and voluntarily set aside days to do without meat, sugar and wheat. Women rolled bandages for the Red Cross, knitted sweaters and socks, ran elevators and took factory jobs once reserved for men. The German-American Trust & Savings Bank changed its name to the Guaranty Trust & Savings Bank.

"The world war will end this morning at 6 o'clock, Washington time," the Associated Press reported November 11, 1918.

By 8 o'clock that Monday morning downtown streets were packed. Vendors sprang up like dandelions, hawking flags, bunting and noisemakers. When motor cars clogged Broadway, Hill, Spring and Seventh Streets, trolley cars were rerouted away from the city's throbbing heartland. Out in Hollywood an eighty-five-foot flagpole went up on a vacant lot at Hollywood Boulevard and Cahuenga. The flags of the United States and its allies fluttered over the foothill suburb.

"The lips of the celebrants were smiling, the heart was bursting with happiness, but the eye was wet with tears," a *Times* reporter observed.

Later, when the statisticians had done their work, they found that 21,761 men had left their homes in the city to serve their country. One hundred and eighty-five had been killed, 189 wounded. On the home front, film stars had helped sell $132,257,000 in Liberty Bonds and moviegoers had become addicted to the Hollywood gossip column.

"Tom Moore," they read the morning after Christmas, 1919, "had bought a Hollywood hill and is building a home thereon. His little daughter will have a whole suite for herself and her nurse; and Mr. Moore will keep a riding horse as well as an automobile."

Chapter 5

The Dizzy Decade
1920-1929

"What Would Jesus Do If He Controlled the Street Railways of Los Angeles?"
—A Sunday sermon topic noted by
LOUIS ADAMIC, 1927.

WHEN FEDERAL Prohibition descended on the land, January 16, 1920, no city in the country boasted a larger membership in the Women's Christian Temperance Union than Los Angeles. The ladies gathered for a day of "praise and prayer," while Al Levy draped his popular Spring Street watering hole in black crepe paper. His customers had anticipated the long dry spell ahead of them by laying in their share of the estimated $1,000,000 worth of illegal booze stashed within the city.

Los Angeles had been legally dry for a little more than six months when the Eighteenth Amendment took effect. The city's experience with the law, the *Times* pointed out, suggested that "the best prophets all seem to have died in time to get written up in the Bible." Temperance leaders, for instance, had predicted that the closing of the saloon would leave police officers sitting around the station house with nothing to do. Instead, it had contributed to an increase in crimes of violence and had introduced "countless" new offenses.

Sailors were smuggling whisky, gin and brandy into the harbor area, and from there the bottles made their way to "blind pigs," where the contents were mixed with water and sold for $20 a quart. The city had lost millions in revenue in liquor licenses and the state's wine industry had been wrecked. In one town "more people died from drinking an imitation booze in one day than were imperiled by the real article in the full length history of the city."

Willard Huntington Wright, like his friend Henry Mencken, had always been more at home in the fleshpots of San Francisco than in the uplifting lecture halls of Los Angeles, but when he traveled north in the early days of the Great Drought, he discovered with dismay that the state's temperance forces had managed to break the spirit of the Paris of the West. The bubbles had gone from its wine.

"No mere virtuous city like Los Angeles, whose piety is indigenous, could ever be so unmistakably, so positively respectable," he reported, and went on to speculate that the difference between the morality of the two cities was "the difference between the virtue of a good man, instinctively generous and upright as a result of early training and environment, and the virtue of a reformed souse, who yesterday was moored to the brass rail, but who today is playing sour notes on a cornet in in a Salvation Army band."

Casting about for some naughty, red-plush remnant of San Francisco's past, Wright stopped by a cafe once noted for its wickedness and fell into conversation with two dispirited women who might have been mistaken for "a brace of lady embalmers."

He left the city saddened by its transformation. "There is something aggressively, inexorably decent and pseudo-elegant about a fallen lady under the pressure of propriety," he wrote, and added a bit of good news for Angelinos. For the first time in California history "the sojourner from Los Angeles is treated with consideration and respect in San Francisco."

* * *

Now that it was assured of sufficient water from the Owens Valley to meet the needs of 2,000,000 people, the *Times* had noted with satisfaction in 1905, Los Angeles found itself "in the novel position of exercising unusual power over industrial affairs and not simply over those within the city, but over even farming and horticulture and gardening operations from the head of the San Fernando Valley to the sea."

The city, in short, had its hand on the faucets of neighboring communities. If they wanted to drink, bathe and water their orange trees, they would have to submit to annexation by the City of Los Angeles. On New Year's Day, 1900, the city's area was 43 square miles. In the fall of 1923, when Ben Macomber of the *San Francisco Chronicle* looked in on the City Planning Commission, he learned that as of that particular day (October 6) the city limits encompassed 391.61 square miles.

"The map of Los Angeles is never completed," Macomber wrote, and found the city "intoxicated with its growth," but "the wise are reinforcing their optimism with caution."

Growth, along with oil-drilling, movie-making and soul-saving, was a major local industry. More people meant more homes and apartments and, thus, more customers for merchants, more deals for land speculators, more mortgages for moneylenders, more jobs for construction workers, and more contributors to the Sunday collection plate. When the real estate market collapsed in 1914, from 10,000 to 15,000 skilled mechanics left Los Angeles to find work in arms factories back East, and the city went through what

Los Angeles High School (upper right) rises above a panoramic portrait of the city's commercial and industrial activity.

a local financier recalled as "six solid years of hell."

In 1920, however, while the rest of the country was suffering from a deflationary hangover, Los Angeles began to perk up. Out-of-work munitions workers headed west with their families, along with drifters and adventurers who had managed to scrape up the downpayment on a flivver, small farmers who had been starved out by falling prices and county seat lawyers and preachers who looked forward to spending their retirement years sprawled in the sun sucking oranges.

"Day after day, the whole week through, month by month, the great stream of humanity is flowing in," the Chamber of Commerce told a *Saturday Evening Post* writer. "There is no end to it. They are coming by train, by boat, by motor vehicle—any way to get here—one ceaseless pilgrimage. From all parts of the world they are coming. No human agency can stop them."

"We'd naturally like it much better if they would mail their money to us instead of coming themselves," remarked a longtime resident who had made a bundle on earlier waves of settlers and would undoubtedly profit from the new migration.

Downtown movers and shakers broke open their best bottles of pre-Volstead liquor on June 10, 1920 to toast the census tabulation which put Los Angeles ahead of San Francisco in population (575,480 to 508,410). "We deserve the honor," crowed a Chamber of Commerce official. Five Angelinos had sprung up where, twenty years earlier, there had been only one, but a businessman boasted that "the real growth of the town has just begun."

"Were you to soar above Los Angeles today in an airplane," *Leslie's* reported, "you would view a city that in area is the largest in the United States. You would see its outstanding features as, first of all, a huge gridiron of wide business and residence streets where thousands of motor cars skim about like great water spiders."

Years later, on a spring day in 1973, when John Pastier, the *Times* architecture critic, climbed into the passenger compartment of the Goodyear blimp and looked down on the city, he found it difficult to believe that "man could urbanize so much land in just a few decades." Except for its inadequate parks and for hillsides that developers had found too costly to mutilate, the only green spaces to be seen were cemeteries and golf courses. The rest of the land had been given over to homes and cars.

"Streets, freeways, parking areas and gas stations occupy perhaps as much space as residences," Pastier noted, "and this automotive domain is rarely pleasant from either the air or the ground."

* * *

"The traffic question has become a problem," the *Times* observed on December 18, 1910, and called on the City Council to do something "to keep the automobiles moving." Ten years later, when Rob Wagner was predicting that undertakers would soon be setting up branch mortuaries at all crossings and wags were referring to Los Angeles as "the city of the quick and the dead," the city fathers came up with a plan to protect pedestrians by outlawing parking in the downtown area.

"The problem before the City Council of making the downtown streets safe for democracy has stirred up a war that makes the Battle of Gettysburg seem like a checker game by comparison," the *Times* observed on January 3, 1920 when the ordinance was being debated.

It took effect the following April, and Angelinos awakened to the realization that, like it or not, they had become dependent on automobiles. A *Times* headline trumpeted the discovery: BUSINESS CAN'T DO WITHOUT THEM. Hollywood came to the rescue of downtown businessmen in the shapely form of Clara Kimball Young, who led a protest parade of cars through the business district. The no-parking ordinance was lifted, except for two evening rush hours. The city had capitulated to the automobile.

"Too bad we cannot make Broadway a three-deck affair," the

Times sighed, momentarily struck by a fantasy which turned the streets over to automobiles, put public transportation underground and had pedestrians walking "on a viaduct level with the second floor of the shop." Fifty years later, dreaming of the Central City of 1990, city planners proposed what they call "pedways" to accomplish the same visionary objective.

"If we are a nation of extremes, Los Angeles is an extreme among us," Sarah Comstock informed readers of *Harper's* (May, 1928). She enjoyed the climate and the carnival atmosphere of the city, admired its new public library, delighted in the Hollywood Bowl's "Symphonies Under the Stars" and, after taking note of this "hurly-burly of speed, noise, light," came to the conclusion that "what Los Angeles is to excess, all our cities are to some extent."

"It suits me beautifully," Louis Adamic declared in a Haldeman-Julius Little Blue Book, *The Truth About Los Angeles* (1927), but in dealing with a city where Christianity ranked as a leading industry (just behind real estate and motion pictures), the author couldn't help being dismayed by a church advertisement listing the topics of a local pastor's next four Sunday sermons: 1.) What Would Jesus Do If He Controlled the Street Railways of Los Angeles? 2.) If He Were A Member of the Los Angeles City Council? 3.) If He Were Owner of a Los Angeles Newspaper? 4.) If He Were District Attorney of Los Angeles County?

* * *

In the early 1920s Angelinos worried about a possible power shortage, grumbled at having some 7,000 schoolchildren on half-day classes, adopted a zoning ordinance, took a spin along a newly opened stretch of Mulholland Drive ("destined to rank with the world's most magnificent drives") and followed the wire service reports from Dayton, Tennessee, where Clarence Darrow represented postwar skepticism in its courtroom confrontation with the Old Time Religion at the "monkey trial" of a twenty-four-year-

Courtesy Security Pacific Bank

Richfield Building, 1920s.

old biology teacher named Scopes.

"My daughter, Myrabel, until a year ago, was attending a private school where the biblical explanation of creation was taught," a *Times* reader wrote the editor. "She was then a righteous and Christian maiden who had the highest ideals. She never smoked or swore.

"Then I sent Myrabel to one of our so-called 'Christian colleges' where she was compelled to study biology and its attending theory of evolution. I should have known better than to send her to these iniquitous colleges. After Myrabel had been taught evolution she no longer had the ideals that were hers before. Her self-respect is shattered. She has bobbed her hair; she uses cosmetics; she smokes and swears. Yesterday she fell so completely into the hands of the devil as to take liquor. I felt compelled to refuse her further admission into our home."

Not only were John Held, Jr. flappers bobbing their hair, painting their faces, smoking, swearing and drinking, they were also turning up their powdered noses at big, old fashioned church weddings. "It is considered much smarter now to be married in a casual, unobtrusive way," a syndicated columnist reported in 1922, and trotted out the testimony of sociologists to confirm what everybody already knew. Parental authority had suffered a mortal setback.

"Similarly," the columnist continued, "the husband's authority over his wife has greatly diminished ... A wife is no longer her husband's absolute property as she was her father's before him.... While in a few States in this country, women still have much the same legal status as they had under the patriarchal regime—which is to say, the status of slaves—throughout the greater part of the United States they are free and equal citizens."

Maiden ladies who, as teenagers, had wondered why an earlier generation had bundled Oscar Wilde off to jail were trying to figure out from newspaper accounts just what Fatty Arbuckle had done to the poor girl in San Francisco ("In the light of his record we find ourselves under the moral necessity of denying him the right to be a public entertainer," the Southwest Chamber of Commerce declared, and called on the Mayor and City Council to prohibit exhibition of his films.)

"Crime," complained a 1927 editorial, "is exploited in the movies until it is become a commonplace and a suggestion of excitement and possible romance. Free love in magazines and movies no longer shocks the sensitive. As a result we reap the whirlwind in divorces and are likely to hold a referendum on marriage itself. Living together has become the black art of tandem polygamy."

God-fearing Angelinos might shudder at the message of modern films and at the morals of their makers, but the industry not only represented a weekly pay roll of $1,500,000 by the mid-twenties, it also drew tourists from all over the world. They drove out to the Fox Studio at Sunset and Western, their autograph books at the ready in case Tom Mix came by, and window-shopped on Hollywood Boulevard, where, they had been told, "movie stars mingle with housewives and society matrons, so decorously garbed that they pass unnoticed on the streets."

Pilgrims found their way to Barbara La Marr's white mansion in Whitley Heights, Jack Holt's cream-colored English lodge in Laurel Cañon, William S. Hart's Sunset Boulevard spread and the nearby estate of Nazimova which later, as the celebrated Garden of Allah, would shelter Robert Benchley and Scott Fitzgerald, among others. Once they reached the Beverly Hills Hotel on their tour of the movie stars' homes, visitors took the advice of a fan writer and turned up "a hill road which leads through iron gates to 'Pickfair,' where dwell filmdom's gracious queen and her athletic husband."

Harry Carr, the *Times* columnist who had known the city since 1887, had watched it grow from 25,000 to 1,000,000. He had seen the handsome residences on Broadway turn into boarding houses and then give way to department stores. He remembered the Baker Block on Main Street near the Plaza when it had been a warren of law offices. Later the block had spawned the city's first fashionable apartments. When their day ended, the rooms had been taken over by penniless writers and artists who, Carr recalled, "gave studio parties and contested as to which could wear the funniest looking hair and talk the loudest."

Carr's memories included not only horse-drawn street cars, but also the city's first yacht-owners and the first two men reputed to be millionaires. "One was John Bradbury, who lived up on Court Street in the first fine house built here. The other was T. D. Stimson, who lived out on Figueroa Street. When we escorted visitors through the town, we showed them these two houses and we said to them with awe: 'He's got $1,000,000.' I don't think any of us really believed it. It was too prodigious. But it was part of looking over the town."

Easterners gaped at signs on recycled bungalows: HOME OF TRUTH and SOCIAL WIDOWHOOD CLUB, laughed at pulpit pronouncements ("If Jesus Christ was on earth today, He would be a Shriner") and went home with snapshots of the Children of the Sun Church, Pre-Astral Fraternity of Love and Nature-Way Medical College for Drugless Healing.

"I leave it to the sociologists to say whether cranks go to California, or Californians become cranks; whatever the process, results are wonderful," Bruce Bliven wrote in *The New Republic* (July 13, 1927) and wondered if someday a "real civilization" might not spring up in this rich, beautiful basin where "today not many civilized persons choose to live."

* * *

In the 1920s, as in the 1880s, newcomers were welcomed to the city by land hustlers. Their buses lay in wait for prospects strolling the north end of Pershing Square. Once aboard, as Will Robinson recalled with relish, they formed a captive audience for spielers who pointed out such local landmarks as No. 56 Fremont Place (where Mary Pickford lived before she married Douglas Fairbanks), the Hollywoodland sign (Mack Sennett was building a million-dollar home on the hill above it) and the Talmadge Apartments (a million-dollar birthday gift to Norma Talmadge from her husband, Joseph W. Schenck).

Inevitably, of course, the spiel bore down heavily on the skyrocketing price of land in Los Angeles. In 1921 memberships in the Wilshire Country Club had gone begging at $100 each. A few years later, because of the increased value of the club's acreage, memberships were worth $5,000. Paramount Studios had bought two blocks in the Sunset and Vine area for $250,000. One was sold in the twenties for $6,000,000.

"Don't Wait!" Janss Investment Company warned in 1923, when it offered lots in Westwood for as low as $950. "A few years ago," the copywriter pointed out, "lots between Western Ave. and Windsor Square—the heart of the high-priced Wilshire District—sold at similar low prices to those of Westwood today. Now they are worth as many thousands as they were hundreds." Prudent investors were advised to "buy on the high lands—away from fog, damp and mists."

By the end of 1924, the boom was petering out, but the *Times*, on New Year's day, 1925, was cheerfully certain that "the actual development of Los Angeles had just begun." To illustrate the dizzying rise of downtown real estate values, the paper traced the history of two lots in a tract the city had given Ozro W. Childs in 1864 for $1 and a promise to dig a *zanja* (ditch) to provide water for the vineyards and orchards in the southern part of town. Childs took title to some thirty city blocks bounded on the north and south by Sixth and Twelfth Streets, and on the east and west by Main and Figueroa.

Ten years later, two lots on the northwest corner of Eighth and Spring Streets, representing only a small fragment of the whole, were sold for $5,000. Twenty years went by and in 1894 they brought $30,000. By 1924 their estimated value was $1,650,000. The owner had picked them up a few years before for $375,000. Thus, in half a century the two lots had appreciated 164,900 percent.

At 4 o'clock on the afternoon of July 15, 1926, the city's book borrowers got their first look at the new public library on Normal Hill.

"Without question one of the noblest buildings in America," tourists were told. "It follows no accented order of architecture, but through it strains of the Spanish, of the East, of the modern European, come and go like folk songs in a great symphony, rising to new and undreamed-of heights in an order truly American in spirit."

Oldtimers took a last nostalgic look at Temple Block ("warped and cracked with years") when it was razed in 1926 to clear space for a new City Hall. The City Council met in its new marble-pillared chamber for the first time on Monday, April 16, 1928. The building ("one of the most distinctive in the world") was formally opened ten days later and councilmen's friends went home clutching a souvenir program.

"There is no particular style of architecture about the new municipal home," the text stated; "it is modern American. . . ."

* * *

Aimee Semple McPherson, 1920s superstar of the salvation circuit, made her way to Los Angeles a few weeks after the Armistice, arriving with $10, a tambourine and a genius for delivering her Happy Road to Heaven sermons in brilliantly staged spectacles. On May 18, 1926 she drove to the beach, changed into a green bathing suit, made some notes for a sermon and vanished while swimming in the warm gentle waters off Ocean Park.

"Aimee is gone," her mother, Mrs. Minnie Kennedy, announced at Angelus Temple the following day. "Pray for her. There is no hope of her coming back."

But in the early morning hours of June 23 a dazed, haggard woman claiming to be the missing evangelist stumbled into Agua Prieta, a Sonora town just across the Mexican border from Douglas, Arizona, gasping out an incredible story of kidnaping, torture

Courtesy Security Pacific Bank

Broadway looking north at Seventh Street, 1926.

and escape. When she came home, she drew a crowd estimated at 100,000, more than had turned out to see the King of Belgium.

"Aimee Semple McPherson was born knowing all there is to know about mob psychology," grumbled the Reverend Robert ("Fighting Bob") Shuler, whose Trinity Methodist Church competed with Angelus Temple for fundamentalist folding money. How, he wondered aloud, echoing questions nagging police investigators and newspaper reporters, had Sister Aimee managed to spend fourteen hours trudging across twenty miles of Arizona desert on a day in late June without working up a sweat, getting sunburned or developing a maddening thirst?

A few weeks later Joe Ryan, a young deputy district attorney, and his father-in-law, Herman Cline, chief of the Los Angeles detective bureau, checked out a cottage in Carmel where a couple passing themselves off as Mr. and Mrs. George McIntire had spent ten days following the evangelist's disappearance. Fourteen witnesses identified the couple as Mrs. McPherson and Kenneth G. Ormiston, a dapper young man who had once run the temple's radio station, KFSG (Kall Four Square Gospel).

"So far as the police are concerned, the mystery of the asserted kidnaping is solved," Cline said, and when District Attorney Asa Keyes (rhymes with "tries") compared the sermon notes Aimee had jotted down on the beach before her disappearance with grocery orders written on paper torn from a pad found at the cottage, he saw no need to submit the material to expert scrutiny, because "any layman can compare the handwriting with Mrs. McPherson's, it is so obviously hers."

Aimee dismissed the incriminating evidence as "a dastardly attempt to assassinate the character and chastity of a defenseless woman." In reply to Fighting Bob Shuler, who was accusing the mayor and city council president of using political pressure to protect her, she asked rhetorically, "Must I permit pastors who preach hate against my creed to lead the hordes of darkness against my church?" Cline and Ryan were brushed aside as a pair of "Catholics persecuting a Protestant minister."

Both men were taken off the McPherson case, bolstering the widespread belief that Sister Aimee would never be brought to trial. A Superior Court judge who presided over a preliminary hearing listened to the conflicting testimony and found "sufficient evidence" to believe that she and her mother had conspired to produce false testimony, but on January 10, 1927, the last day on which the district attorney could legally proceed with the prosecution, he came into court and asked for a dismissal of the case.

"My story is as true today as it was the first time I told it," Aimee assured her followers at one of the darkest moments of her seven-month ordeal, and when it was over, she set out on a cross-country "vindication tour." The *Times* expressed its relief that the district attorney had finally brought to a "welcome, if ungraceful, conclusion an episode which has served no other purpose than to make a laughing stock of Los Angeles."

* * *

In the spring of 1927, while Aimee and her flock roasted marshmallows on the beach at Ocean Park, celebrating the first anniversary of her disappearance and miraculous resurrection 550 miles inland, a young air mail pilot was keeping an eye on North Atlantic weather reports, hoping to pick up the $25,000 prize awaiting the first aviator to fly nonstop from New York to Paris, and in Philadelphia a wealthy seventy-seven-year-old book collector lay dying.

Charles Lindbergh's joyous reception in Paris shared front-page attention in Los Angeles, May 24, with news of the death of Henry Edwards Huntington, who had defected from San Francisco in 1902 to build for Angelinos the world's finest mass rapid transit system. He had spent the last seventeen years of his life gobbling up the most notable libraries within reach of his checkbook.

"I am going to give something to the public before I die," he told his San Marino ranch superintendent in the spring of 1906, and thirteen years later, when he had come to be known as "the greatest figure in the history of American book-collecting," he signed a document setting up an institution "to promote and advance learning, the arts and sciences, and to promote the public welfare by founding, endowing and having maintained a library, art gallery, museum and park."

The flag over City Hall flew at half-mast and Leslie Bliss, curator at the Henry E. Huntington Library and Art Gallery told reporters: "Great book collectors have come and gone, but it has been given to no one of them to amass in so short a time, less than twenty years, in fact, a library so renowned as that assembled in its own building on its founder's well-loved San Marino ranch."

"This is like heaven to me, " he once remarked to a friend, and two generations of scholars and tourists have shared his enjoyment of his home, his library and his gardens.

In that same spring of 1927 Ralph Bunche, a twenty-two year old political science major, was mulling over a suitable subject for the commencement address he was to deliver at the old Vermont Avenue campus of the University of California, Southern Branch. His philosophy professor lent him a copy of Edna St. Vincent Millay's poems and suggested he repair to the beach to read, reflect and "mellow" his soul.

"The world is periodically scourged and scarred by fiendish wars," he pointed out nearly a quarter of a century before he won the Nobel Peace Prize, and he went on to tell his fellow-seniors, "The future peace and harmony of the world are contingent upon the ability—yours and mine—to effect a remedy."

As an undergraduate Bunche had been denied membership in a debating society because he was black. Several members resigned in protest and formed an organization of their own, the Forum. He was elected its treasurer and proceeded to win a gold medal in an Inter-Forensic Society oratorical contest.

"Undeniably," he declared in a 1926 competition, "the people of the world today are inextricably bound together by bonds of common interest which make imperative an effective, active international organization."

By the time he died in December, 1971, he had become, in the words of United Nations Secretary-General U Thant, "the most effective and best known of international civil servants." "Above all," observed a writer for the *Times*, where he had once worked as a delivery boy, "he demonstrated and elevated the dignity of man."

* * *

Bill Mulholland, a lanky, sharp-tongued Irish immigrant who came ashore at San Pedro in 1877 and got a job as a *zanjero* (ditch-tender) with the privately owned Los Angeles City Water Company, was guest of honor at a 1927 Department of Water and Power banquet observing the silver anniversary of municipal ownership. Mullholland had been asked to stay on as superintendent in 1902 when the city acquired title to its distribution system. In the next three years he cut domestic bills in half.

"I went to school in Ireland when I was a boy, learned the three R's and the Ten Commandments—or most of them—made a pilgrimage to the Blarney Stone, received my father's blessing, and here I am," he said when asked how a man with no formal training as an engineer could hold down his job. He dismissed a proposal that he run for mayor by saying he would "rather give birth to a porcupine backwards."

His St. Francis Dam, built in a canyon some twenty-odd miles north of Los Angeles, doubled the city's storage of Owens River water and saved the San Fernando Valley's crops in the drought year that followed its completion in 1926. Two cracks appeared on the face of the dam in January, 1928, and were calked. Some weeks later, on the morning of March 12, Mulholland and his chief assistant, Harvey Van Norman, drove up to the dam to inspect a new leak. They saw no cause for alarm and headed back to the office, arriving in time for a late lunch.

At 11:57 that night the dam collapsed. Twelve billion gallons of water raged through the rich Santa Clara Valley to the sea at Ventura, sweeping aside homes, automobiles, livestock, orange groves, bridges and highways. More than 400 men, women and children were killed.

"I envy the dead," Mullholland groaned and took full responsibility for whatever human error of judgment might have been made.

He resigned that fall, as work was beginning on a bold new plan to tap the Colorado River for a supply of water four times greater than could be delivered by the Owens Valley aqueduct. Work on the project was stopped for a minute of silence when Mulholland died in 1935. He had seen Los Angeles grow from a village of 15,000 to a city of nearly one and a half million people. The semi-arid basin he irrigated can best be seen today from the magnificent scenic drive that bears his name. There is also a Mulholland memorial fountain at Los Feliz and Riverside Drive, near the site of the one-room shack where the young ditch-tender schooled himself.

* * *

When Winston Churchill finished speaking at a Metro-Goldwyn-Mayer luncheon, September 28, 1929, the toastmaster said it was such a brilliant talk he would like to hear it again. Whereupon, as the Los Angeles *Examiner* reported next day, "the magic of the talking motion picture's marvelous advance was invoked." Churchill's words had been picked up by a microphone hidden in a bouquet of flowers on the table.

The *Examiner* was struck by the machine's ability to reproduce "word for word, tone for tone, an address which had the moment before charmed you with its pleasantry, its wisdom and its prophetic import." A few months earlier the Fox Film people had announced that all of their future pictures would be "talkies," and predicted that "many screen favorites will lose out under the new policy." When the *Times* asked its readers, "Do you prefer talking pictures to silent films?" fifty-six percent said, "No."

Mrs. Christine Sterling, executive secretary of a civic-minded outfit called Plaza de Los Angeles, Inc, was fighting to preserve some remnants of the pueblo's past by saving the Avila Adobe from destruction and closing Olvera street to vehicular traffic. She got her proposal through the city council without a dissenting vote, only to have it vetoed by Mayor John. C. Porter, an Iowa-born dealer in used cars. The council overrode his veto on September 3, the day before the city's one hundred and forty-eighth birthday.

As the decade ended, downtown merchants were following their customers in the city's westward movement. In September, 1929, Bullock's opened its Wilshire branch "in recognition of the growing needs of a great city" and Silverwood's moved to the Miracle Mile, just across the street from Desmond's. In a single generation, Silverwood's had drifted south on Spring Street from the 100 to 200 block, and then over to Sixth and Broadway before settling down on the recently reclaimed grain fields of Wilshire Boulevard.

"Westward the star of business takes its way," sang the *Times*.

All the while, however, the downtown skyline continued to be dominated by height-limit buildings. Twenty-three went up in 1926, twenty the following year. The Richfield Building, completed in 1929, was described as "an expression of modern art and thought." The architects (Morgan, Walls and Clements) had not only air-conditioned the entire building, but had arranged for its five passenger elevators to whisk motorists from the garage level to their offices. Bullock's-Wilshire, giving the automobile the same deference, had provided for a popular new service feature, off-street parking.

In late October, 1929, some 500 brokers, bankers and local functionaries assembled at 618 South Spring Street to watch a giant steam shovel, acting on a signal from the Mayor, break ground for the new $1,500,000 Los Angeles Stock Exchange. A week later the market collapsed.

Courtesy Security Pacific Bank

The "Hot-Rodders" convene on the edge of town (9th and Broadway).

Chapter 6

Depression and "A Dream of Empire" 1930–1939

> *"Señorita Los Angeles yesterday morning threw wide the doors to her one hundred and fiftieth birthday party with colorful ceremonies upon the wide steps of City Hall."*
> —*LOS ANGELES TIMES*, September 5, 1931.

THE CITY'S cuffs might be frayed and its bank account overdrawn, but to Mayor Porter, the used-car dealer who had declared war on Communists and bootleggers, the Depression was merely a temporary deviation from a divine master plan for the metropolitan area.

"The situation is not at all alarming," he assured his constituents. "We do not find it necessary to feed our unemployed men here. In San Francisco I saw free soup kitchens. There are none here."

In Los Angeles, as Duncan Aikman explained to readers of *The Nation*, "official confession of community distress is regarded as a heresy to the cult of boosterism." Thus, the feeding of down-and-out Angelinos was turned over to missions in the slum sections. A veteran missionary, chosen "the most useful citizen of Los Angeles," received a medal from the city fathers, only to have the muckraking *Los Angeles Record* sniff out the disclosure that he was serving decayed restaurant garbage. The mission asked the restaurants to provide more palatable scraps and the city's most useful citizen kept his medal.

"Why don't they take all that money and give employment with it or feed the poor?" malcontents grumbled when the city drew up plans for a ten-day fiesta to mark the one hundred and fiftieth anniversary of its founding.

As usual, the *Times* was standing by with an answer. The birthday party would "spread the fame of Los Angeles far and wide and bring in a harvest of tourists." Also, "this backward look through history, emphasizing as it does the difficulties which Los Angeles has overcome in becoming the city of today, puts present difficulties in perspective." The fiesta would help lift the city out of the commercial doldrums by lifting its spirits. As everyone knew, "much of the Depression is psychological."

The blonde granddaughter of a Yankee banker reigned as queen of the fiesta. Mayor Porter got himself up as a ranchero and Governor James (Sunny Jim) Rolph, Jr., resplendent in black and gold, with a bright sash around his paunch, appeared to a *Times* reporter as "the true pioneer leader." Douglas Fairbanks, riding at the head of the motion picture contingent, "looked every inch a caballero." General Andres Pico was portrayed by a man named Murphy and Leo Carrillo played Leo Carrillo, the city's ceremonial Latino.

"This city has no money to waste on senseless decorations, flags, rodeos and other schoolboy stunts," Loren Miller complained in the local black paper, the *California Eagle*. "We are facing a winter in which hundreds of poor and destitute men, women and children will go without adequate food, clothing, and shelter."

Some 10,000 spectators, uncomfortable in the hot, late summer sun, jammed the Plaza for a reenactment of the myth-makers' conception of the pueblo's founding. Four acolytes in white surplices and red cassocks, carrying a cross and candles, led a procession of soldiers, priests and settlers. Eleven white couples, with twenty-two white children in tow, represented the black and brown *pobladores* who had come north from Mexico to establish the settlement on the banks of the Porciúncula.

A choir of forty male and female voices brought a lump to the throat of the *Times*. "If the spirits of those first inhabitants of El Pueblo were near, the strains of *When at Thine Altar*, a chant ascribed to the Cathedral of Cologne in 1623, must have sounded pleasingly familiar to their ears." More likely, the spirits of the settlers would have been wondering what had happened to their complexions.

"Those who saw the parade, and we have been assured that few Negroes did," the *California Eagle* declared, "must have a sense of the utter childishness of a race so saturated with prejudice that it attempts to change the color of its founders' skins . . . ."

At 1:35 A.M. on the pueblo's birthday, Major James H. Doolittle left Burbank and touched down at Newark, New Jersey, eleven hours and fifteen minutes later, setting a new transcontinental plane record. Next day, crossing the continent in the opposite direction on the Chief, Rudy Vallee's bride arrived in Los Angeles and was asked about life with the celebrated radio crooner. "Just an ordinary man," she replied.

Aviation and romance melded again at the close of the fiesta. Six planes of the California National Guard dropped high explosives on a mock-village near the airport, only to be upstaged by Aimee Semple McPherson. Attractively turned out in one of "the new Eugenie hats and a modish blue suit trimmed with blue fox fur," she slipped off to Yuma, Arizona, in a chartered tri-motor plane and returned to Angelus Temple as the bride of a chubby young choir singer.

"God has rolled away my lonesomeness," purred Mrs. David L. Hutton.

Bride, bridegroom and mother-in-law ("My darling deserves the best in life") took up four columns of the *Times*, leaving only one for the National Guard's preview of the destructive force of military aircraft. The pilots were hailed as "symbolic of all that is modern."

* * *

During the fiesta, someone rooting through the archives at the Title Guarantee and Trust Company dug up a letter written to the City Council by Major Henry Hancock* on a summer day in 1854. The pueblo's population at that time had been less than 1,600, but to the Mexican War veteran, a surveyor by profession, the shape of its future could already be determined.

"Los Angeles is no longer the quiet, peaceful and happy abode of rancheros alone—its slumber is over—an impetus has been given her, she has assumed another character, is becoming a commercial mart, a nucleus around which are rallying all of the concomitant enterprises of a prosperous and flourishing inland city."

Speaking as "a surveyor of the innumerable and inviting valleys which surround you," Major Hancock urged city councilmen to stop disposing of city lots indiscriminately and to give some thought to securing common property "for the comfort and undivided enjoyment of the community at large." The letter turned up at a time when Angelinos were pleading for parks and public beaches, while the city continued to spread out in whatever direction land speculators found profitable to take it.

During the last decade the city had been engulfed in a human tidal wave. In 1920, with a population of 576,677, Los Angeles had ranked as the country's tenth largest city. Ten years later,

* Hancock Park is named for his son, who gave the Pleistocene animal trap to the county in 1915.

with a population of 1,238,048, it was fifth. Looking back fifty years to a period when the city had been "the stepchild of the Pacific Coast," huddled on a desert, "scantily supplied with water and power, out of the track of progress," the *Times* attributed this prodigious growth to a single factor, the city's faithful adherence to "the American Plan or open shop principle of industrial relations."

Only by waging a relentless fight against "the militant aggressions of unionism" had this inland seaport managed to surpass San Francisco, the editors claimed. Forty years earlier, the manufactured products of San Francisco had been thirteen times as valuable as those of Los Angeles. By 1927 the Southern California stepchild had forged ahead by a three-to-two margin. Any backsliding from the open shop gospel, the *Times* warned, would cause the city's growth to "slow down, stop or even reverse its direction."

Los Angeles, in one generation, had shot up from a small town to a city to a metropolitan community, but its new urban dimensions had brought back the pueblo's ancient fear of a water famine. At the time city fathers first hit on the idea of tapping the Owens River, the local water supply had been about 72,000 acre-feet a year. By 1931 it was approximately 280,000 acre-feet, and history was repeating itself. Again the area's population had caught up with its available water resources.

"The growth experienced during the last quarter of a century cannot be duplicated in the same length of time—or ever, for that matter—if additional water is not obtained," the *Times* pointed out during the city's anniversary fiesta, when voters were mulling over a proposed $220,000,000 bond issue to bring water from the Colorado River to the cities in the metropolitan area.

The project was even more ambitious than Mulholland's Owens Valley aqueduct. Water was to be carried 242 miles from a lake below Hoover Dam to a reservoir from which it would have to be channeled another 150 miles to the borders of the cities in the Metropolitan Water District. Work began in the depths of the

Depression, when the first President from California (he had, of course, been born in Iowa) was preparing to turn the White House over to the Democratic Governor of New York, who had promised to cut down on government spending.

While downtown businessmen were plumping for passage of the Metropolitan Water District bonds, a conservative lawyer-banker, Jackson A. Graves, noticed a curious deterioration in the city's "matchless climate." On week-day mornings, when he left his home in Alhambra, the air was "fresh, pure, clean and invigorating," but when he got to the Central City, his vision was "impaired by dust, smoke, and the infinitesimal, invisible excrescences which arise from the crowded and much traveled streets and sidewalks. To me, the breathing of this atmosphere is extremely disagreeable; it gives me congestion of the head and nasal passages."

* * *

On December 4, 1931, just three months after the pueblo kicked off its birthday celebration, the *Times* took note of its fiftieth anniversary by publishing a two-part supplement. One harked back fifty years to the day when "there appeared on the doorsteps of a sleepy, little frontier town on the edge of the desert, a few hundred copies of a four-page newspaper," and the other described the world of 1981, as viewed by such distinguished contributors as:

Lee De Forest: "Television sets will be in every modern home."

Douglas Fairbanks: "When you go into the theater of the future, it will be just as though you were sitting in this room as I am now. The screen will be big enough for your eye to rove about on it and come back to the main action."

Sir Oliver Lodge: "We will be communicating with our departed dead."

The Very Reverend William R. Inge, Dean of St. Paul's, London: "The rational costume for both sexes—cheap, becoming and scanty—will enable beauty to be recognized in the body and limbs as well as in the face."

Owen Johnson, writing on the liberated woman: "She will lay down the terms on which she will reproduce the race."

Dr. R. A. Millikan: "When coal and oil are gone, science will find a way to utilize the energy of the sun."

Sir James Jeans: "It may be that science will in time discover how to transform atomic energy into power. If this vision is realized, even partially, the curse which fell on Adam will be lifted, and heavy manual labor will almost disappear from life."

Henry Ford: "Public charity will be an ancient dream and no longer a reality."

Albert Einstein: "Enlightened peoples will learn to abhor war and refuse to participate in it."

Eric Temple Bell: "By 1945 Prohibition will cease to be an issue. Substitutes for gin, with forty times the potency and no ill effects, will be on sale at soda fountains."

William B. Stout: "One can leave New York after breakfast and arrive in Los Angeles in time for evening dinner."

Learned men foresaw a brave new world of television and transcontinental flights, a world free of wars, welfare, hangovers and unwanted children, but, reviewing the predictions a generation later, nothing seems wider of the mark than Bryant Hall's prizewinning essay on life in Los Angeles in 1981.

The city fathers, in Hall's vision of the future, had done away with downtown parking, billboards, power poles and overhead wires. Public buildings in the new Administrative Center were tucked into what appeared to be "an enormous park or garden, traversed by broad, tree-lined avenues." Thanks to farsighted city and county planners, Angelinos roamed freely along beaches from Santa Monica to Laguna, "nearly all publicly owned."*

Commuters and sightseers moved around the metropolitan area on "the finest system of urban and interurban transportation ever developed." No one ever had to wait more than thirty seconds for a bus.

---

* "Southern California's greatest single resort asset—the public beaches—is slowly but surely diminishing in size," the *Times* warned on August 15, 1926 in a feature article headlined: COUNTY'S BEACH PLAYGROUNDS PASSING TO PRIVATE HANDS.

Such was the dream in 1931. The reality was reported by a *New York Times* correspondent: "The city has no subways, its bus lines and its street car systems are hopelessly inadequate, if you want a taxicab you must telephone and then wait until a driver can be waked up and sent forth."

* * *

Statistically, in this city of immigrants, every other Angelino pinching the beefsteak tomatoes at the new Farmer's Market had been living somewhere else less than five years earlier. In the crowds outside Grauman's Chinese Theater, hoping to catch a glimpse of Clara Bow or Nancy Carroll at the premiere of a new talking picture, only a few old duffers could remember when Hollywood was a bone-dry rural community where retired shopkeepers sat in the shade of pepper trees wondering what the folks back home in Kansas were up to.

Some of the new Angelinos managed to live comfortably on the return from income property, others had struck it rich in oil or real estate. By their religious fervor in converting a tolerant, loose-living pueblo into a respectable, palm-shaded replica of their hometowns, all had contributed to Southern California's celebrated incongruities.

"The man with the hoe," Lillian Symes wrote in *Harper's* (June, 1931), "the horse trader, the crossroads storekeeper, the small-town evangelist may have dignity and fitness in his native setting. But dwelling in pseudo-tropical bungalows equipped with every modern gadget, playing horseshoes in shirtsleeves and suspenders beside a dazzling sea, disporting himself at Home State picnics under the eucalypti, inveighing against tobacco and the sins of the flesh in the shadow of the eternal mountains, he becomes slightly grotesque."

A new race of godlike creatures ("the men are bronze Apollos, the girls are golden Venuses") had been spawned by the "toil-worn, penny-saving peasants who, on a windy Kansas prairie, heard of the Garden of Eden and came west to invest in its real estate." While the old folks shambled off to Angelus Temple to hear Sister Aimee or to Trinity Methodist Church, where fighting Bob Shuler thundered against saloonkeepers, pornographers, white-slavers, political connivers and his sexy Echo Park rival, young native Angelinos, born to sun and surf, headed for the beaches and the tennis courts.

It came as no surprise to Miss Symes that California athletes were conquering the world. "They are bigger, better and handsomer," she wrote, quite undone by "so much perfection in hair, teeth, skin and line." At times, after ogling young Ronald Colmans and Joan Crawfords darting down high school steps and playing miniature golf, she felt as though she had entered a "private playground set aside by the Hollywood studios for the picked choruses of the current musical talkies."

Twenty years had passed since the invasion of Hollywood by movie-makers. They had stumbled into the peaceful community of Christian teetotalers like a party of drunken convention delegates mistaking a vesper service for a stag film showing. By 1930, when the making of motion pictures had become as important to the local economy as drilling for oil and turning chaparral-covered hillsides into tract homes, most of the actors and the studios had moved away, but for tourists, it was enough to walk the same paved streets where their silent screen deities had disported themselves before they moved on to Beverly Hills or Forest Lawn.

Mildred Adams, sketching the pueblo's portrait for the *New York Times* in the summer of 1930, was struck by the cultural clash of white Anglo-Saxon Protestant Hollywood and the Plaza, where Mexicans lived cheek-by-jowl with Chinese, Japanese, black and indigent whites in "a dark, crowded section, hot and thick, as full of mysterious ingredients as chili con carne, and as quick to burn." The Plaza was "a hotbed of vivid, violent life, as fertile as Hollywood is sterile."

Hollywood, for Robert Benchley, was "the dullest and most

conventional community of its size in the country." Among its other deficiencies was an absence of speakeasies, "as the refined elements in other communities know speakeasies." The Plaza, for Aldous Huxley, was a fascinating "slum of Africans and Filipinos, Japanese and Mexicans. And what permutations and combinations of black, yellow and brown! What complex bastardies! And the girls—how beautiful in their artificial silk!"

While thousands of unemployed Latinos drifted south to Mexico, back-country farmhands from Georgia, Alabama and Mississippi continued to pour into the city. The black population climbed from 2,131 in 1900 to 38,894 in 1930. The newcomers lived apart from their white neighbors, concentrating in frame houses along Central Avenue, where the best jazz in town could be heard at the Dunbar Hotel. A black deputy city attorney was in line for a Municipal Court vacancy in the fall of 1932, but at the last minute Governor Rolph decided against the appointment. He quoted Calvin Coolidge who, in a similar situation, had said: "Let the people establish the precedents. It is not for me to establish the precedents."

* * *

"It hit hard in Los Angeles," Matt Weinstock later wrote of the Depression. "The unemployment and relief rolls were in the tradition of the biggest and best; but during those bad years, while things were at half speed, people rediscovered the city. They couldn't afford night clubs, or the fancy places, so they went to the zoo at Griffith Park. They ducked Palm Springs and the High Sierras in favor of a picnic in Mint or Bouquet Canyon, or their back yards. The economic pressure taught them a great lesson: a person couldn't have his malnutrition in a nicer place than Los Angeles."

While the unemployed sunned themselves in Pershing Square and hungered for bread, the city fathers gave them a circus, the Tenth Olympiad. A million-dollar Coliseum designed to seat

75,000 spectators went up on state land in Exposition Park and, for another million, its seating capacity was boosted to 105,000, making it the world's largest sports arena. Every seat was taken when the games opened on July 30, 1932, and when they closed on August 14, leaving only three previous Olympic records unbroken.

"This idea of the athletes of the world living together as neighbors will go a long way toward promoting world peace," said the secretary of the Netherlands Olympic Committee after visiting Olympic Village.

Japanese athletes were not swept off their feet by Los Angeles. The streets and buildings, they were surprised to find, were no more modern than those of Tokyo, and some were inferior. They were also dismayed by their hosts' casual dress. "Thousands thronged the city coatless and many without their neckties," they told the *Japan Times* when they returned home.

At the games, they reported, they had been treated fairly and courteously by officials and by spectators, but in the evening, when they had set out to dine in one of the city's better restaurants, they had been turned back at the door with the curt explanation, "Mexicans are not admitted." "We are not Mexicans, we are Japanese," they had explained, only to discover that this made matters worse.

"Most disgusting of all," continued the *Japan Times* story, "was the fact that the second generation Japanese and those resident in California took such a situation for granted...."

* * *

Shortly before Christmas, 1931, Angelinos read a syndicated article by Adolf Hitler, "leader of the National Socialist Party of Germany, popularly known as the Nazis," who expressed his determination "to give Germany back to the Germans" and predicted that "spring is surely coming to our poor, unhappy Germany." Fifteen months later, on an early spring day in 1933, an

Associated Press dispatch reported: "Germany became a dicta-. torship under the old Prussian system today, the Reichstag handing over to Adolf Hitler the power to govern by decree for the next four years."

In Washington that day, March 23, Franklin D. Roosevelt was beginning the third week of his Administration's first one hundred days, Long Beach was digging out from under a devastating earthquake and up north, in Berkeley, the sixty-five-year-old University of California was giving an honorary degree to Walter Lippmann.

"The old order of human affairs is gone, irrevocably so," he said. "In the new order the loose, individualistic and acquisitive democracy of the nineteenth century will be replaced by a much more highly integrated, socially conscious form of government."

Californians gave this new order of human affairs a spectacular laboratory test when Upton Sinclair, the prolific Socialist muckraker, hit on the idea of "production for use" and took it to the electorate in a gubernatorial campaign remarkable for the venom, duplicity and sheer terror it produced in an opposition that linked Harry Chandler and William Randolph Hearst, Louis B. Mayer and Aimee Semple McPherson Hutton.

"The factories were idle and the workers had no money," Sinclair recalled in his autobiography. "Let them be put to work on the state's credit and produce goods for their own use, and set up a system of exchange by which the goods could be distributed."

On September 1, 1933, without telling anyone, not even his wife, Sinclair changed his registration from Socialist to Democrat. Mrs. Sinclair, he said later, gave him a mighty dressing down," but when he entered the Democratic primary the following year as a candidate for governor, he won easily, collecting nearly half a million votes. His campaign manager came up with a name for his messianic movement, EPIC—End Poverty in California (or, as the opposition put it, Empty Promises in California).

"The fundamentalist, revivalist religious nature of Upton's campaign would be fascinating to reporters who later came from the East in large numbers to cover it," Leon Harris wrote in his biography of the "Isiah in pince-nez."

A reporter for the *New York Times* described the "quiet, slight figure, with a pleasant smile constantly on his lips, suggesting inner certainty rather than humor or political winsomeness." A *Collier's* writer was impressed by the fervor his "world-old-gospel of the underdog" inspired in his audiences. "Under another influence," the article suggested, "they would have greeted Aimee Semple McPherson Hutton as she wafted whitely across her platform in Angelus Temple a few miles away. Or the Reverend Billy Sunday as he bounded to his pulpit croaking his homely anathema upon forty-seven devils."

Sister Aimee attacked "the red devil" by exposing her flock to some of the shocking things he had written in *The Profits of Religion*. The passages read aloud in her temple, it turned out, were simply Sinclair's paraphrasing of the words of her Savior. If elected, readers of the *Los Angeles Times* were warned, Governor Sinclair would "sovietize California and destroy her business and industry by confiscatory taxation and the competition of land and factory communes."

Louis B. Mayer turned his Culver City studio into the unofficial headquarters of the film industry's organized campaign of vilification and misrepresentation. He wangled a day's pay from Metro-Goldwyn-Mayer employees and put them to work on Irving Thalberg's fake newsreel interviews with bewhiskered actors voicing their enthusiasm for EPIC in Russian accents. The most effective footage focussed on Central Casting hobos huddled on the borders of California, waiting to live off the bounty of its taxpayers once Sinclair got elected. Political leaders, the *New York Times* declared later, attributed his defeat (1,138,620 to 879,537) "to the splendid work on the part of the screen."

"How would California be different if you had won in 1934?" a reporter asked nearly a quarter of a century later, when Sinclair was approaching his eightieth birthday.

"We did win," he replied. "We gave California and all the other states an exciting awareness of what democracy really is. F.D.R. was listening to us. And a young district attorney in Alameda County was listening. A fellow by the name of Earl Warren."

* * *

Toward the end of a routine workday in the late 1930s, Earl Warren lumbered into the office of Helen MacGregor, his personal secretary, and said he had to make a speech on the Bill of Rights.

"He dictated some notes," Miss MacGregor said years later, "taking each of the rights and telling how it hampered him as district attorney. But then he went on to say that he wouldn't have any one of those rights diminished in any degree 'for my sake, my children's sake, or my children's children's sake'."

About the same time, in the late spring of 1938, when Warren was preparing to run for attorney general, his first state-wide political campaign, he lunched with Superior Court Judge Robert W. Kenny, a prominent Los Angeles Democrat, and asked for his support.

"It would be a lot easier for me if you'd make some kind of statement on civil rights," Kenny said, and a few weeks later he received a handwritten letter from the Alameda County district attorney expressing the belief that "the American concept of civil rights should include not only an observance of our Constitutional Bill of Rights, but also the absence of arbitrary action by government in every field and the existence of a spirit of fair play on the part of public officials toward all that will prevent government from using ever present opportunities to abuse power through the harassment of the individual."

Three days later Earl Warren received the endorsement of Bob Kenny, who was raising money for the state's Democratic ticket headed by Culbert Olson. In the August primary Warren won the nomination of both parties and ended up as a Republican attorney general serving as legal advisor to a Democratic governor. "The greatest single nuisance" facing the new attorney general in Southern California when he took office, January 2, 1939, was a fleet of four gambling ships, making blatant use of newspapers, radio stations and billboards to lure local sports to their illegal tables.

"This ship is operated by courageous, open-minded, fearless American citizens," said Antonio Stralla, alias Tony Cornero, who commanded the fleet's flagship, the *Rex*.

Warren launched his attack on Friday evening, July 28, when some 800 customers had taken water-taxis out to the *Rex* for an evening of cards, dice, roulette and bingo.

"It was like a military operation," recalled Warren Olney III, assistant attorney general in charge of the criminal division. "Since we had only five investigators in our office, we had to use deputy sheriffs from the county of Los Angeles. We knew that many of them were in the pay of the gamblers, so Earl ran the whole thing with the utmost secrecy to avoid a tip-off to the ships. On D-Day, we locked up forty cops and eight accountants in Patriotic Hall in Los Angeles, and Earl briefed them. Then we transported them to the waterfront in sealed buses, and loaded them directly into waiting patrol boats from the state Fish and Game Authority. The raids went off like clockwork. I later became an officer in the Marine Corps, but I always remember my experience with Warren's Commandos as my first amphibious operation."

Olney took command of the task force dispatched from San Pedro to subdue the *Tango* and the *Mount Baker*, anchored off Long Beach. Oscar Jahnsen, Warren's chief investigator, left from the Santa Monica pier to board the *Rex* and the *Texas*. Warren, along with the sheriff and the local district attorney, directed the operation from a beach club command post on a bluff overlooking the sea. It was equipped with telescopes and shortwave radiophones.

The startled skippers of the *Tango* and the *Mount Baker* quickly capitulated. "My God, cops!" Olney heard one man cry out. "And they're not ours!" The *Texas* also surrendered without a fight, but the *Rex* turned its fire hoses on the seafaring posse and blocked the gangway with heavy steel doors.

"All right," Warren instructed Jahnsen by radiophone, "if they won't let us on, we won't let anyone off. It's a process of attrition. They've got women aboard whose husbands don't know they're out gambling, and they've got husbands aboard whose wives don't know they're out with other girls. Let's see what happens."

"I won't give up the ship," Cornero was quoted as saying, but after holding out for ten days, he surrendered unconditionally. Warren climbed into a Fish and Game patrol boat and rode out to the *Rex*.

"It was like General Grant taking General Lee's sword," Olney remembered.

Cornero was brought ashore shortly before noon and booked at the Santa Monica police station. Asked to give his occupation, he replied: "Mariner."

* * *

Television was still "a laboratory affair" when M. H. Aylesworth, president of the National Broadcasting Company, visited Los Angeles in 1934. "There are probably only one hundred receiving sets worthy of the name in the country," he told reporters, and predicted that television would mark "the next great step in world communication." Within three years it was being used by Little Orphan Annie's Daddy Warbucks to keep in touch with his Singapore office.

"Television history is to be made today when KHJ inaugurates a series of weekly television sound broadcasts, synchronized with the broadcast of images from W6XA0, the Don Lee television station, at 7:30 P.M.," the *Times* reported September 9, 1936, and by the end of the decade KHJ's radio programs were reaching an audience of 8,000,000, compared to the 1,500 or so television enthusiasts who could bring in W6XA0 on their homemade sets.

On a spring morning in 1934 C. C. Julian gulped a fatal potion of poison in a Shanghai hotel, a year after jumping $25,000 bail in Oklahoma. His death revived memories of a massive 1920s stock swindle that siphoned some $50,000,000 from the savings of small investors, rocked Spring Street with the indictment of more than forty prominent citizens and resulted in the imprisonment for bribery of District Attorney Asa Keyes.

When the *Times* moved into its new building at First and Spring Streets in the summer of 1935, Will Rogers served as master of ceremonies for a half-hour radio program featuring Kitty Carlisle ("vivacious songbird of the musical comedy realm") and Bing Crosby ("silver-throated crooner"). Rogers joked about the old Broadway building having been infested by a new breed of termite, the daily columnist.

He flew to Seattle a few weeks later and set off on a leisurely flight around the world with Wiley Post, who had twice circled the globe. On August 15, making their way from Fairbanks to Point Barrow in an Arctic fog, their red monoplane crashed as it took off from a river bank. A startled Eskimo ran fifteen miles across rain-soaked tundra to carry the news to Point Barrow.

"One of the princely wits and kingly characters of the age," said Darryl Zanuck, vice president of Twentieth-Century Fox.

As the 1930s drew to a close, Angelinos recalled Mayor Frank Shaw and replaced him with Judge Fletcher Bowron. Charlie McCarthy was chosen grand marshal of the 1940 Tournament of Roses, which was to be seen for the first time on television. Los Angeles County was still the country's leading agricultural county, but it was also producing more than half of its airplanes as well as its most monumental traffic jams.

"Imagine driving your car on an exclusive express highway through the congested Los Angeles metropolitan region at a constant speed without a stop or hindrance," the Automobile Club of Southern California purred in a report urging the construction of a 400-mile network of divided motorways, four to six lanes wide, serving a 2,000-square-mile area. The cost was estimated at $800,000,000.

Stop-and-go signals make a brave stab at controlling Spring Street traffic.

The decade closed with Angelinos celebrating two historic achievements, completion of the Union Passenger Terminal and the main line of the Colorado River Aqueduct. A generation later, the railroad station would be empty, the Colorado River water supply inadequate, and local breadwinners would be lining up for unemployment benefits because the flow of money from Washington for space travel had slowed to a trickle.

Half a million Angelinos turned out on May 3, 1939 to have a look at the new railroad station across from the Plaza. It was the "most modern terminal in America," they were told, and in all the excitement over its formal opening, nobody bothered to check the industry's economic pulse. In the last ten years the railroads had laid off half of their employees and two-thirds of their total mileage was in serious difficulties or bankrupt.

Six months later, on November 19, cool, clear water from the Colorado River traveled 242 miles through tunnels, open canals, conduits and siphons from Lake Havasu to Riverside, where it would be stored until it was carried another 150 miles to the other cities of the Metropolitan Water District.

"It is a dream of empire coming true before our eyes," said W. P. Whitsett, chairman of the district's board of directors.

With the aqueduct splashed across the front page, little attention was paid to a brief wire service story filed from Berkeley: "Dr. Ernest O. Lawrence, 38-year-old University of California professor who recently was awarded the Nobel Prize in physics, announced tonight he has been asked by the University of Texas to continue his atom-smashing experiments there."

Courtesy California Historical Society

Enemy alien, 1942

Chapter 7

War and Peace
1940 – 1949

"After four frantic years of war and four wild years of peacetime boom, it is plain that Los Angeles will never be like anything else on earth."
—*TIME*, July 4, 1949.

MATT WEINSTOCK was on record against Sunday driving (" a form of madness"), but on Sunday, December 7, 1941, he drove his wife, Hilda, down to Puente, where friends had a walnut ranch. Not until the Weinstocks got home that afternoon did they hear about the bombing of Pearl Harbor.

"A neighbor told us as we got out of our car." Matt wrote in his *Daily News* column. "This is unimportant except that people may remember in years to come exactly what they were doing the day

Japan attacked the U.S."

Kenji Nakauchi, Japan's slight, bespectacled young consul, with a son of high school age back home, learned of the air raid while out for a walk.

"I knew the situation was serious, but I didn't know it was this serious," he told reporters who came to his door at 7425 Franklin Avenue, and when pressed for a comment, he threw up his hands. "What can I say except that I am quite sorry?"

There were some 40,000 residents of Japanese ancestry in the Los Angeles area, he estimated, and they were about evenly divided between Issei (those born in Japan) and Nisei (those born in the United States). The consul saw no reason why either first or second generation Japanese should be taken into custody. He cited his experience in Vancouver, where he had been stationed at the time Canada went to war with Germany and Italy.

"All the Germans and Italians were not locked up," he said.

Little Tokyo was stunned, but its cafes, bars and newsstands stayed open. "We will obey the law," an elderly Issei remarked, and went on watering plants in front of his florist shop. A middle-aged neighbor found it hard to believe that the Japanese Government had ordered the attack. "Couldn't it be possible," he speculated, "that Germans might have, in some manner, got hold of Japanese planes and carried out the bombing?"

Harbor officials quarantined the Japanese fishing fleet and when the *S.S. Catalina* docked at Wilmington, an agent of the Federal Bureau of Investigation was on hand to scrutinize the sightseers. In its efforts to leave no subversive stone unturned, the FBI descended on the Zamorano Club, only to discover it was a goodly fellowship of politically conservative book collectors who had named their organization after California's first printer, Agustin Zamorano (1798-1842).

* * *

A yellow signal, indicating the approach of enemy aircraft went out over the state-wide police teletype at 7:55 P.M., Wednesday, December 10. Six minutes later, KFI, the city's key radio station in times of emergency, announced "a complete blackout immediately from Bakersfield to San Diego and as far east as Boulder City and Las Vegas." All other radio stations went off the air.

Shortly after eight o'clock Fire Department sirens sounded for one minute and street lights winked out. Air raid wardens traipsed through the darkened streets, warning housewives to douse the lights of their Christmas trees and drape blankets across their windows. Pedestrians fumbling their way home were bowled over by motorists driving without headlights. Every ambulance at the city's command was pressed into service.

All next day Angelinos were bombarded with radio warnings of a trial blackout set for 9 o'clock that night, but two hours before the city was to turn off its lights, the test was cancelled. Suddenly at 9:42, however, an Air Raid Warning Service yellow light flashed the message: "Raiding party on the way." After an hour's confusion as to whether they were being subjected to a test or a possible air attack, Angelinos heard the all-clear and tumbled back into bed, only to be awakened at 2:50 A.M. by another alarm. Local radio stations went off the air and the city waited for the enemy planes that never showed up. The all clear sounded at 4 o'clock.

Ordinarily police would have expected an average of twenty-five burglaries and five robberies during the period of the blackout. Instead there had been no burglaries and only three holdups. One person had been arrested, a recalcitrant drunk who had refused to extinguish the lights in his house.

* * *

The blackout that still sticks in the memories of middle-aged Angelinos, the mysterious battle of Los Angeles, took place in the early morning hours of February 25, 1942. The stage was set on February 23, when a Japanese submarine, I-17, surfaced near Santa Barbara and pumped thirteen rounds of 5½-inch shells into an oil installation at Ellwood.

Next evening, around 7 o'clock, the Navy received warning from Washington of an impending attack on Los Angeles. Five hours later the military's then-secret radar screens picked up an unidentified target about 120 miles west of the city. At 2:27 the object appeared to be only three miles away. At 3:06 something resembling a balloon was sighted over Santa Monica and antiaircraft batteries were ordered to open fire.

"The gunfire brought everyone to a window or front porch," *Newsweek* later recalled. "Golden tracers arched upward in the blackness. More than 1,400 three-inch shells were fired. Shrapnel whistled down to clatter on hard pavement or imbed itself in yards and houses. But no bombs were dropped."

The Army had been shooting at clouds, the Secretary of the Navy suggested, but the Secretary of the Army stood firm on his statement that unidentified planes had, indeed, appeared over the city. Although Lieutenant General John L. DeWitt, commanding general of the Western Defense Command, thought it "possible" that the aircraft had been launched from a Japanese submarine, he considered it "more likely" that they had been civilian planes operated by unauthorized pilots.

A spokesman for the Japanese Navy joined the debate in the fall of 1945. No Japanese planes had flown over Los Angeles during the war, he said, and only one had taken off from a submarine surfacing near the West Coast. It had circled above southern Oregon on February 9, 1942, with orders "to attack military installations but the lone plane was unable to discover any."

On the twentieth anniversary of the "battle," a *Times* reporter in Washington burrowed into the federal archives, hoping to clear up the mystery. Official records, he found, were so confused and contradictory that it was impossible to reconstruct the story, and, a classified document added, "the subsequent testimony of eyewitnesses, both civilian and military, complicates rather than clarifies them."

* * *

On the eve of their first wartime Christmas, Angelinos checked their supplies of candles and flashlight batteries, laid in an extra bag of sugar and stayed within reach of their radios. Bob Hope spent Christmas with his family. Robert Taylor and Barbara Stanwyck entertained the Jack Bennys in their new Beverly Hills home. Corporal Jimmy Stewart was at Moffett Field and Mickey Rooney was planning to marry an eighteen-year-old actress from North Carolina named Ava Gardner.

In the first seventy-two hours after the Pearl Harbor attack, FBI agents had rounded up 316 Japanese, 73 Germans and 11 Italians. By Christmas, when local jails bulged with suspected fifth columnists, their wives, parents and friends were pleading with United States immigration authorities for permission to visit the prisoners, many of whom were American citizens.

"They are being well fed and kept comfortable—and if found innocent of any connection with the enemy, they will be released," an immigration official explained to the press, and cheerfully added: "Meanwhile, we are showing them how democracy works."

* * *

"A hell of a thing, especially for an American citizen," Tom Ikkanda, a service station owner on Olympic Boulevard, grumbled to himself when he first heard rumors that concentration camps were being prepared for Japanese-Americans.

On February 19, 1942 President Roosevelt issued Executive Order 9066, authorizing the designation of military areas "from which any or all persons may be excluded." Little Tokyo bristled with signs, CLOSING OUT SALE. Some offered discounts up to fifty percent on their belongings; others simply asked prospective buyers to make an offer.

The first contingent of Japanese Angelinos, aliens and citizens alike, left for the hastily built evacuees' city of Manzanar on March 21. American children wearing Superman tee-shirts and Shirley Temple frocks were carted off to the Owens Valley with their parents and grandparents. No wrongdoing had been charged or proved. Guilt no longer had to be established in a court of law according to prescribed procedures. Now it could be inherited.

"We're charged with wanting to get rid of the Japs for selfish reasons," a spokesman for Salinas Valley growers and shippers told a *Saturday Evening Post* stringer. "We might as well be honest. We do. It's a question of whether the white man lives on the Pacific Coast or the brown man."

* * *

"Race does not lie in the language but exclusively in the blood," wrote Adolf Hitler, and, in the summer of 1942, his Berlin radio station was happy to quote similar sentiments expressed in a report prepared by the Los Angeles County sheriff's office, setting forth the official explanation of juvenile delinquency in the Mexican-American *barrios*.

"The Caucasian, especially the Anglo-Saxon, when engaged in fighting, particularly among youths, resorts to fisticuffs and may at times kick each other, which is considered unsportive; but this Mexican element considers all that to be a sign of weakness, and all he knows and feels is a desire to use a knife or some lethal weapon. In other words, his desire is to kill, or at least let blood.... When there is added to *this inborn characteristic* that has come down through the ages, the use of liquor, then we certainly have crimes of violence." (Emphasis added.)

Violence, in short, was presumed to be in the liquor-heated blood of these brown-skinned youngsters whose forebears had founded the pueblo which now excluded them from so many public parks and pools, theaters, dance halls and restaurants, but not from selective service.

"We are Americans for the draft, but Mexicans for jobs and the police," young men complained.

This generation of Mexican-American Angelinos had sprung from the Depression years, when the city's Spanish-speaking shops and cafes were drifting away from the Plaza, inching south as far as Third and Fourth Streets, engulfing ten-cent stores and movie houses along the way.

"Being strangers to an urban environment," Carey McWilliams points out in *North From Mexico* (1948), "the first generation had tended to respect the boundaries of the Mexican communities. But the second generation was lured far beyond these boundaries into the downtown shopping districts, to the beaches, and above all, to the 'glamor' of Hollywood. It was this generation of Mexicans, the *pachuco* generation, that first came to the general notice and attention of the Anglo-American population."

The *pachuco* adopted as his uniform the "drape-shape" or, as it was called outside the *barrios*, the "zoot-suit." To the police, inflamed by the sight of the pleated, peg-topped, high-waisted trousers and the long, loose, wide-shouldered coats, the bizarre costume identified young gangsters who, from time to time, had to be rounded up and worked over.

In August, 1942, when the body of young José Díaz was found in the vicinity of an abandoned gravel pit near Slauson and Atlantic Boulevards (a local newspaperman dubbed it "The Sleepy Lagoon"), police arrested twenty-four young Mexican-Americans, including two who had signed up with the United States Navy. On January 12, 1943, twelve of the defendants were found guilty of murder and five of assault.

The evidence against them was so flimsy that their convictions were overturned by the District Court of Appeal, but not before eight of the young men had served nearly two years in San Quentin. Corridors of the Hall of Justice swarmed with exultant families, friends and neighbors on the late October day in 1944 when the prisoners were set free.

"For the first time in the history of Los Angeles," wrote Carey

McWilliams, who served as chairman of the Sleepy Lagoon Defense Committee, "Mexicans had won an organized victory in the courts and, on this day, bailiffs and deputy sheriffs and court attaches were looking rather embarrassed in the presence of Mexicans."

In the meantime, while the Sleepy Lagoon youngsters were still behind bars, trouble had broken out in Venice between *pachucos* in "drapes" and some teenage Anglos reinforced by sailors spoiling for a fight. "The only thing we could do to break it up," a police officer later recalled, "was to arrest the Mexican kids." Inflammatory reports in the local press ("guerilla gang warfare," "youthful terrorists," "juvenile hoodlums," "reign of terror") helped make an explosion inevitable.

It was sparked on the night of Thursday, June 3, 1943, after eleven sailors walking along the 1700 block of North Main Street were set upon by what they described as a gang of zoot-suiters. Next evening some two hundred sailors took over a fleet of taxicabs (how they found the cabs remains a mystery) and invaded the east side *barrios*, leaving four youths lying on blood-stained pavements. Nine sailors were arrested, but no charges were ever brought against them.

The Army and the Marine Corps joined the Navy in the following night's assault. Arms linked, the servicemen stormed the downtown streets four abreast. Civil and military authorities obligingly looked the other way, but when some young Mexican-Americans gathered on a street corner, they were promptly packed off to jail. On Sunday, June 6, sailors beat up eight *barrio* teenagers and wrecked a bar on Indiana Street. The police made forty-four arrests. All were Mexican-American and all had been badly mauled. The *Daily News* account was headlined:

44 ZOOTERS JAILED IN ATTACKS ON SAILORS

On Monday night, a mob of several thousand servicemen and

civilians swarmed over the Central City, halting street cars and breaking into theaters, dragging *pachucos* out into the streets, stripping them naked and beating them senseless. It was a Mexican version of the Chinese Massacre of 1871, and it lost little in the translation. Local authorities, then as earlier, not only made no serious effort to stop the bloodletting, some even joined in the evening's sport. Al Waxman, editor of *The Eastside Journal*, described an incident he witnessed at Twelfth and Central.

"Four boys came out of a pool hall. They were wearing the zoot-suits that have become the symbol of a fighting flag. Police ordered them into arrest cars. One refused. He asked: 'Why am I being arrested?' The police officer answered with three swift blows of the night-stick across the boy's head and he went down. As he sprawled, he was kicked in the face. Police had difficulty loading his body into the vehicle because he was one-legged and wore a wooden limb. Maybe the officer didn't know he was attacking a cripple.

"At the next corner a Mexican mother cried out, 'Don't take my boy, he did nothing. He's only fifteen years old. Don't take him.' She was struck across the jaw with a night-stick and almost dropped the two and a half year old baby that was clinging in her arms...."

"Most of the citizens of the city have been delighted with what has been going on," beamed the *Eagle Rock Advertiser*, echoing the pueblo's vigilante past, and County Supervisor Roger Jessup might well have been draped across the Bella Union bar in the 1850s knocking back a shot of rye whisky with Major Horace Bell when he delivered himself of the opinion, "All that is needed to end lawlessness is more of the same action...."

* * *

Roger Butterfield snapped a candid portrait of Angelinos at war on an assignment for *Life* (November 22, 1943). "We get four crops from our Victory Gardens," he was told by a backyard farmer, who also delighted in being able to "go swimming any day in the year." Paddock Engineering Company had orders for more than 1,000 postwar pools, and livewires at Forest Lawn were preparing a helicopter field "to receive funeral processions from the air."

"I never dreamed there was such a place," a North Dakota soldier had told one of Butterfield's informants. "I'm coming back here to live after the war."

The young civilian soldiers streaming through Union Passenger Terminal caught a glimpse of blue skies and palm trees, sniffed the exotic odors of Olvera Street, hitchhiked out to the Hollywood Canteen to dance with drama majors from Iowa and flew off to the South Pacific dreaming of a postwar life built around beach parties at Malibu and backyard barbecues in the Hollywood Hills.

While the GIs were writing V-mail letters from bomb-torn atolls, a European philosopher of history, Paul Schrecker, took a brief, horrified look at Los Angeles (somebody tried to sell him an "Idealistic Hamburger"). "The city seems not like a real city resulting from natural growth," he decided, "but like an agglomeration of many variegated movie sets, which stand alongside one another but have no connection with one another." Writing in *Harper's* (September, 1944) at a time when the word "smog" was just coming into common usage, he predicted that the boom town "might soon become the most populated place in the world—or a ghost town just as well."

Two years later, when Angelinos got the Christmas issue of *Newsweek*, they found most of one page taken up with a report on their smog. Nobody knew where to fix the blame ("dumps, lumberyard incinerators, locomotives, diesel trucks, an asphalt plant, and oil refineries" were leading candidates), but everybody suffered from the acrid fumes and the city's boosters were squirming over a headline in the *St. Louis Globe-Democrat*:

BEAUTIFUL, SUNNY CALIFORNIA, EH?
LOS ANGELES NOW NO. 1 SMOG TOWN

* * *

The war officially ended at 4 o'clock, Los Angeles time, Tuesday, August 14, 1945. The siren on top of the *Times* building screamed the news to downtown shoppers and office workers, touching off a monumental traffic jam. Servicemen kissed every girl in sight, including the plain ones, and many of the babies born that day were to go through life as Victor or Victoria. Mayor Bowron intruded a sobering note on the carnival.

"Peace," he pointed out, "threatens industrial dislocation in this area which might throw thousands out of work."

Los Angeles, "the arsenal of democracy," was still the seat of the nation's richest agricultural county, but by the end of the decade, as *Time* reported in a cover story (July 4, 1949), its economy no longer rested on oil fields, citrus groves, film studios and aircraft plants.

"It lands more fish than Boston or Gloucester, makes more furniture than Grand Rapids, assembles more automobiles than any other city but Detroit, makes more tires than any other city - but Akron. It is a garment center (bathing suits, slacks, sports togs) second only to New York. It makes steel in its backyard. Its port handles more tonnage than San Francisco."

In an earlier day, asthmatic druggists and dairymen had moved to Los Angeles to take the sun and pick oranges from their own trees. Now Rexall Drug and Carnation were moving their corporate headquarters to Los Angeles, joining the city's new generation of veterans and defense workers. It was impossible to build enough schools and hospitals, install enough telephones, provide enough sewers and parking lots. The overgrown pueblo had become a prisoner of its own technological wonder-working.

"The good Lord didn't intend this to be an industrial city," the mayor declared, adhering to the downtown tradition of linking the city's development with celestial planning.

Whatever providence may have intended for the Los Angeles basin, the City Hall observation deck on a clear day in 1949 commanded a view of thousands of acres of smoke stacks, assembly plants, warehouses, refineries and processing plants, interspersed with new factory towns sheltering the families of migrant workers who had come to the metropolitan area to find jobs in defense plants and had stayed on to plague city officials with their demands for schools, hospitals, libraries, parks and playgrounds.

"For the past fifteen years," Carey McWilliams wrote in *Harper's* (October, 1949), "the city has shown the incompetence of an idiot giant in dealing with its affairs. The story of this vast city's bungling of such problems as traffic, transportation, spoiling of its beaches, the sewage, smog, and related items would make a monumental municipal comedy of errors."

Westchester illustrated his point. In 1940 it had been open country, much of it planted in lima beans. By the end of the decade, some 30,000 people, most of them young, were living in Westchester. The city had no fire or police stations, no emergency hospital facilities, not even a barber shop. Its library was "about as big as a boxcar" and its elementary schools consisted of "hastily thrown together bungalows." Nothing had been planned. Like the child of a summer cruise romance, the city just happened.

The prologue to the metropolitan area's postwar difficulties had been recited six weeks before the attack on Pearl Harbor, when city planners and architects took over seven galleries of the Los Angeles Museum of History, Science and Art for an exhibition contrasting what the metropolis had become and what it might be.

"A topographic panorama showed visitors what a beautiful place Los Angeles County had been before the Angelinos had got there," *Time* reported. "Other panoramas depicted the idyllic cattle and sheep ranches of a century or more ago, the land and oil booms of the 1880s and '90s, the leaning fences and signboards of the 1920s. The 1941 display pictured children playing in congested streets, oil wells blossoming on front lawns. A weather-beaten shack, transplanted whole from a Los Angeles slum, stood accusingly before a backdrop of Los Angeles' sky-

A young Pachuco, *stripped of his "zoot suit," comforts a riot victim.*

scraping city hall."

In the city planner's projection of their future, Angelinos lived in a spacious, sun-drenched world where homes and factories were separated by recreational greenbelts, where poverty had been swept from view and cars sped safely along one hundred miles of projected parkways (only fifteen miles of which had actually been built).

Less than a year earlier, on December 30, 1940, the West's first freeway, a six-mile stretch of "miracle boulevard," had been thrown open to the public. The Arroyo Seco Parkway* had made Pasadena a twelve-minute drive from downtown Los Angeles. Compton, as city planners liked to point out, was the same distance from the Central City—nine miles—but the trip took thirty-five minutes. In the 1941 exhibition, "...Now We Plan," the city's future was committed to the automobile and the freeway.

In a reflective mood six years later, when Angelinos were observing the one hundred and sixty-sixth anniversary of the pueblo's founding, a *Times* editorial writer took note of the price the city had paid for its wartime growth. "Industrial expansion has created smog and attracted hordes of people—it may be too many people," the editorial declared. "The change from an easy, pleasant place to live has come on us suddenly, amazingly. We have not had the time to plan the city's future."

Meanwhile, the big red cars of the Pacific Electric Railway Company, which had served and, in large measure, shaped the metropolitan area, had become an endangered species. It was front-page news, March 1, 1949, when the state's Public Utilities Commission was asked to approve a plan to replace 200 trolleys with 200 buses on 11 of PE's 17 streetcar routes as part of a $4,500,000 "modernization" program.

"The need in Los Angeles today is for more and better rapid rail transit, rather than abandoning what we have and adding to our serious street traffic management problem," Bowron pointed out.

"Los Angeles County," as the *Times* saw it, "is not exactly like

* Its name was changed to the Pasadena Freeway in 1954.

any other urban area and must work out its own optimum combination of rail and rubber transportation."

The city was still groping for the combination a generation later when Larry E. Moss of the Sierra Club remarked to a local reporter: "I suppose we should not condemn those original planners so much because they could not foresee the adverse effects of the freeway. But we should chastise those who, in the 1950s and 1960s knew better and, knowing better, still continued to buy the cloudy visions."

* * *

If one day in the life of the postwar metropolis could be brought back for dissection by some urban pathologist probing for the early warning symptoms of the city's present disorders, February 6, 1947 might serve as well as any other. It was a warm, winter day, when the smog was somewhat worse than usual. There was a slight earthquake some one hundred miles distant at 9:30 that morning and the nation's airlines were bruising their backs with self-congratulatory slaps at having come up with a noise abatement program. In Sacramento, oil and trucking lobbyists had managed to beat down Governor Earl Warren's highway improvement bill.

"Every month of delay will mean we will continue to have at least 300 people killed and 6,000 injured, many unnecessarily," the Governor snapped, and took off for Washington, where he was to testify on behalf of water development and flood control in the Central Valley.

The temperature in downtown Los Angeles had hit 80° the day before and a twelve-foot, cigar-shaped torpedo had fallen on Burbank from a military plane. A more generous sugar ration stamp, good for ten pounds, would soon be available. It reminded Matt Weinstock's readers of the remote day in 1942 when Angelinos had gone to their neighborhood elementary schools to sign up for ration books and a Beverly Hills matron, asked how much sugar she had on hand, had replied, "Three lumps."

Police were running down another false lead in the Black Dahlia murder case. Mae West was making a personal appearance at the Biltmore Theater and *The Drunkard* was in its fourteenth year. Moviegoers could choose among *The Best Years of our Lives*, *The Jolson Story* and *The Razor's Edge*. Catholic students had called a mass meeting in the hope of launching a month-long boycott of movie houses to protest the current wave of obscene films.

In its daily box recording the previous day's "smoke" conditions, the *Times* noted that visibility at the Civic Center had been cut from ten miles at 10 o'clock in the morning to two miles by midafternoon. "To a person who knew Los Angeles in her better days," said one of the doctors in town for a rheumatic fever conference, "this smog is most regrettable. It makes for more respiratory irritations—which in turn tend toward more respiratory diseases. These lead to more rheumatic fever."

"It's impossible," Evelyn Waugh grunted when reporters followed his spoor to the Bel-Air Hotel and asked for an audience. Betty Crocker was celebrating her silver anniversary with Gold Medal Flour and Sonny Wisecarver, having run off at the age of fourteen with a twenty-one-year-old housewife and two years later with another married women, this one nine years his senior, had bobbed up in Las Vegas, where he hoped to find work and get married. The eighteen-year-old paramour had his eye on a girl of sixteen.

A generation after General Otis had gone to a non-union grave, Charles E. Wilson, president of General Motors, was telling a Senate committee that he would take up farming rather than submit to a union contract. The Dow Jones industrial average had hit 182.52, the highest level in five months. Eddie Arcaro had brought in two winners at Santa Anita and Babe Ruth, on the eve of his fifty-third birthday, was "feeling fine." Rear Admiral Richard E. Byrd was puttering about the South Pole and Margaret Truman had moved out of the White House and taken an apartment in New York.

While Republican Congressmen were trampling the grave of Franklin D. Roosevelt by supporting a proposed constitutional amendment limiting presidents of the United States to two terms, Representative Helen Gahagan Douglas ("the gentlewoman from California," as the Speaker called her) made the shocking statement that "more families are homeless in Los Angeles today than after the San Francisco earthquake or the Johnstown flood."

An estimated 162,000 families, including 50,000 veterans, were holed up in tents, garages, cabins, trailers and firetrap hotels. After reminding her colleagues that they had appropriated two billion dollars during the war years to run up cantonments, Mrs. Douglas pointedly asked, "Do you have to go to war to get a roof over your head?" Her eloquent plea on behalf of her Veterans' Emergency Housing Bill didn't make the *Times* next day, but space was found on the front page for a wire service story on a Florida cold wave.

*The Dodgers in Los Angeles for the opening day parade,
Friday 18 April 1958.*

Chapter 8

Getting Into The Big Leagues 1950-1959

"It's the first time Los Angeles ever had a chance to become anything."
—THE NEW YORKER, 1959

LOS ANGELES, in 1950, was well on its way to becoming the nation's third largest city or, as some insisted, the world's largest parking lot. Its air was foul and its traffic congested, but the county's air pollution watchdogs were confident that by summer they would reach "the turning point in the war on smog" and the state's freeway builders were counting on their superhighways to move Angelinos about the basin at a merry clip.

By the time the decade ended, however, the air was more

noxious than ever, the freeways were clogged and Mayor Bowron had been swept from office by a colorless, *Times*-backed Congressman, Norris Poulson, who attacked the incumbent for his failure to provide a mass rapid transit system, a charge Poulson's successor would be fielding twenty years later in an unsuccessful bid for a fourth term

"The most American of all American cities," Hamilton Basso decided when he visited Los Angeles on an assignment for *Holiday* (January, 1950), and, with a slight shudder, took note of "a growing school of thought that it might very well be on its way to becoming the greatest of all American cities."

Basso marvelled at its newness ("most of what is now Los Angeles—seven-eighths of it, to be exact—has grown up in the past thirty years"). He looked in on the Sunset Strip, dined at Chasen's and Romanoff's, visited the harbor, noted the deficiencies of the local transportation system ("can't even begin to meet the demands placed on it") and paid a ceremonial visit to Forest Lawn ("a country club for the dead").

Once he had sorted out his notes and impressions, he added up the city's faults and virtues ("its belief in newness and bigness, its addiction to fads, its hope for the future, its willingness to try anything once, its idealistic pragmatism, its cultural gropings and materialistic grain") and came to the conclusion that he was looking at "our national character writ large."

The diagnosticians who, like Mr. Basso, dropped by from time to time to see what the inmates were up to in the country's largest open-air asylum generally came from New York, a city swollen by quite a different stream of immigration. The New York melting pot had boiled and bubbled for generations with huddled masses of Europeans yearning to breathe free. Southern California, on the other hand, had been overrun by shivering midwesterners aching to warm their arthritic joints in the winter sun.

The Europeans had come to the New World with empty pockets to build a new life. The Midwesterners had come to the New Eden with the profit they'd turned by selling the farm or the feed store, enough to tide them over until they died with a healthy tan. In New York, the emigrés had sought to better their lot in life by joining a labor union and the Democratic Party. In Los Angeles, the newcomers looked to the Republican Party, the Protestant ministry and the *Times* to see that their savings and their way of life were protected from welfare chiselers, Communists and One Worlders.

"What happened to the Okies who migrated to California during the Depression?" Mayor Poulson was asked in 1955.

"They've become Republicans and drive Cadillacs," he replied.

* * *

In 1979, when Jeanne Parry, a Scandinavian Airlines system publicist, looked back twenty-five years to the company's first polar flight from Los Angeles to Europe, she discovered that gasoline cost twenty-seven cents a gallon in 1954. Eggs were thirty cents, steak eighty cents a pound. A young couple starting a family could get a 4 percent mortgage on a two-bedroom house selling for $10,000. Jerry Brown was a tenth grader at St. Ignatius High School and Ronald Reagan was starring in *Cattle Queen of Montana*.

"It was the day of ducktails, poodle cuts, Elvis, bomb shelters, beatniks, 3-D movies, Hula Hoops, the Edsel and Bridey Murphy," Anne Welsh, a Los Angeles free-lance writer, recalled, and Ginger Timmons Ludwick reminded *Times* columnist Jack Smith that "all a girl needed to take to college was a trunkful of skirts, two drawerloads of lambswool or cashmere sweaters, a Peter Pan collar dickey, white bucks and a ballet-length formal."

Angelinos, in the 1950s, debated the desirability of building backyard air raid shelters, read *Peyton Place*, explored the city's new pizza parlors, watched the Kefauver and McCarthy hearings on television, detected the scent of marijuana floating above the beatnik pads of Venice and, on the historic morning of October 1, 1957, found themselves required, under a penalty of a $500 fine and a six-month jail term, to abandon their incinerators in favor of trash cans.

Bathtub tenors sang *Three Coins in the Fountain*. The tobacco industry came out with filter-tip cigarettes and pay phones demanded a dime instead of nickel. School children practiced air raid drills and, in 1955, lined up for injections of Jonas Salk's new polio vaccine. During the next quarter of a century the number of Americans stricken with poliomyelitis shrank from around 40,000 to something in the neighborhood of twenty. In the meantime, children no longer had to brace themselves for the needle. They were taking Albert Sabin's oral vaccine in a cube of sugar.

On Monday, July 18, 1955, just three months after the first polio vaccine was declared safe, the parents of seven-year-old Michael Schwartner of Bakersfield and five-year-old Christine Vess of North Hollywood managed to place their children at the head of a line of 15,000 people waiting to buy tickets to Disneyland when the ten turnstiles opened at 10 A.M. The two families were greeted by Walt Disney, who gave them lifetime passes to his new Anaheim playground.

"It started with my taking my two kids around to zoos and parks," Disney explained. "While they were on the merry-go-round riding forty times or something, I'd be sitting there trying to figure out what you could do that would be more imaginative."

When they weren't stuffing telephone booths or staging panty raids, college students read J. D. Salinger, Jack Kerouac and *Playboy* (Marilyn Monroe was the first Playmate). Draft cards were tucked into billfolds rather than thrown into bonfires. Fifty-four thousand young Americans were killed in Korea, while Senator Joseph McCarthy and the House Un-American Affairs Committee ripped open the national woodwork in search of subversives.

"Light is the one thing the Communist species of vermin cannot stand, and publicity is one of the most effective ways a free society has found to control them," the *Times* noted in welcoming HUAC to the city in the fall of 1952. The paper placed itself solidly behind John Wayne's campaign to "delouse" Hollywood. The exterminators figured there were only about one hundred "actual, hard-bitten, revolutionary Communists" among the film colony's thirty thousand members.

"You've got to place McCarthy in proper perspective in your own life," Mort Sahl pointed out, "because eventually you'll have to tell your kids about him—unless you want them to learn it in the streets."

Mort Sahl, a 1950 graduate of the School of Public Administration at the University of Southern California (his degree was a B.S.), went to work at Enrico Banducci's San Francisco night club, the hungry i, in December 1953. Once word got around the campus grapevine that an irreverent new political messiah had arisen in the Bay Area, he moved on to clubs in Los Angeles, Chicago and New York. Wearing a sweater, his collar open at the throat, his hands fiddling with a rolled-up newspaper, he was the Eisenhower Era's back-of-the-hall heckler.

After Chief Justice Warren spoke for a unanimous Supreme Court in declaring that separate-but-equal classrooms were unconstitutional because "separate educational facilities are inherently unequal," Sahl told his cover-charge constituents that President Eisenhower had come out strongly against slavery, "except in certain remote areas when farm labor isn't available."

When television cameras focused on white parents, screaming and shaking their fists at nine black children signed up for classes at Central High School in Little Rock, Arkansas, someone suggested that the President take a Negro girl by the hand and lead her past the barricade of bigots.

"That's easy to say if you are not involved," Sahl commented. "But if you are in the Administration, you have a lot of problems of policy—like whether or not to use an overlapping grip."

* * *

Federal troops were standing watch over Central High and Milwaukee baseball fans were heading for the third game of the

Courtesy Security Pacific Bank

Congestion and pollution come to the conjuntion of Spring and Main Streets in the 1950s.

Braves-Yankees World Series on Friday, October 4, 1957, when the Soviet Union announced the launching of Sputnik, history's first earth satellite. The 184-pound sphere, with a diameter of twenty-three inches, was circling the globe every ninety-five minutes.

"The White House insisted today that the Soviet's launching of an artificial moon was no surprise to the U.S. Government," Robert Hartman, chief of the *Los Angeles Times* Washington Bureau, reported. "President Eisenhower, golfing at Gettysburg, had no immediate comment."

Three days later, when the Tass news agency reported the successful testing of "a mighty hydrogen warhead," Angelinos were huddled in front of their television sets as the City Council debated a controversial deal to bring the Brooklyn Dodgers to Los Angeles by swapping a decrepit minor league ballpark in a run-down neighborhood for 300 acres of undeveloped land in Chavez Ravine a couple of miles from the downtown district and close to the city's freeway network.

"I would like to see a National League team move to Los Angeles," Walter O'Malley, the shrewd, affable president of the Brooklyn Dodger organization, said in 1954, and predicted that a pennant contender could draw three million fans a year.

Two years later, when attendance at Ebbets Field had dropped nearly 600,000 from a 1947 high of 1,807,000, O'Malley may have noticed a brief United Press story in the Sunday *New York Times* reporting the results of a special census which had placed the population of Los Angeles at 2,241,433, strengthening "its claim to being the nation's third largest city." The following February he acquired the Los Angeles Angels and the team's home grounds, Wrigley Field.

O'Malley met with Mayor Poulson and County Supervisor Kenneth Hahn at the Dodgers' spring training camp in Florida a few weeks later to discuss the possibility of transferring the team to a handsome new stadium in Los Angeles with 50,000 seats and acres of parking space. In Brooklyn only 700 cars could be parked and 32,000 customers seated. Poulson and Hahn came home with a Vero Beach tan and glad tidings, "We've got the Dodgers."

"Now Los Angeles is major league in every sense of the word," Poulson said on October 8, 1957, after rounding up the tenth City Council vote he needed for approval of the transaction. He showed reporters a telegram from O'Malley: "GET YOUR WHEELBARROW AND SHOVEL. I'LL SEE YOU AT CHAVEZ RAVINE."

The city had acquired its Chavez Ravine acreage from the Federal Government with a proviso that it be used for "public purposes." Critics of the Dodger "giveaway," as they persisted in calling it, objected to turning the land over to a money-making organization in a deal which left the city stuck with a shabby ballpark in an undesirable location (it was razed in 1964) and called for the expenditure of nearly five million dollars in public funds for grading operations and access roads.

The city, in addition to Wrigley Field, was promised $60,000 a year for twenty years to maintain a recreational facility that was never built on a forty-acre parcel across from the Police Academy. O'Malley's real estate taxes, at the time he made the deal, were estimated at $350,000 a year. They rose to more than a million dollars before his death in 1979, but the city got no cut on the Dodger gate receipts, parking fees, or concessions. To keep thirsty fans from foregoing a contribution to the national pastime O'Malley put no drinking fountains in his $20,000,000 stadium. They had to be added later.

"Win or lose, they belong to Los Angeles and the city will cherish its own," the *Times* declared, April 18, 1958, when the Dodgers arrived for their first game in their new home. The subway rivalry between Flatbush and the Bronx, now transplanted to California, resulted in a 6-5 victory of the Los Angeles Dodgers over the San Francisco Giants. The crowd at the Coliseum (78,672) was said to be the largest turnout for an opening day game in big league history. A visiting New Yorker was impressed by the fans' enthusiasm. "They even applauded foul tips," he told a friend that night.

But 51,767 spoilsports had signed petitions calling for a referendum on the Chavez Ravine deal. This issue was to come before the voters on June 3. As the *Times* saw it, the question to be resolved was whether Los Angeles was to become "a great city, with common interests," or "continue its degeneration into a geographical bundle of self-centered sections." In short, a yes vote on the construction of a modern, major league stadium in "a sort of half-forgotten wilderness in the very center of the metropolitan area" would be interpreted as a "declaration that Los Angeles shall be a city, not just an aggregation of suburbs."

The Dodger deal prevailed by a narrow margin (25,785). Passions cooled considerably during the next season when the home team won the National League pennant and the 1959 World Series. The ardor with which Angelinos embraced the Flatbush Bums caught the worldly eye of *The New Yorker*.

"While Brooklyn used to hold the Dodgers in affection, Los Angeles seems to hold them almost in awe," the magazine noted, and after quoting Louella Parsons to the effect that Eva Gabor had "added to the excitement of the World Series yesterday by getting married," its editorial spokesman went on to say, "It appears that the Dodgers have given the land of make-believe something real to cling to. 'It's not our feelings about baseball that have us all stirred up,' one reasonably old-time settler said the other day. 'It's that this cockeyed, sprawling place has finally had a chance to become a unified city. It's the first time Los Angeles ever had a chance to become *anything*.' "

* * *

As the 1950s opened, Angelinos owned 354,000 television receivers, most of them purchased in 1949 because of lower prices, better programming, a subsiding fear of obsolescence and a relentless advertising campaign. A twenty-eight-page section of the *Times*, March 8, 1949 trumpeted the debut of KTTV (Kall Times Television), the joint property of the Times Mirror Company (51 percent) and the Columbia Broadcasting System (49 percent).

"In its traditional eagerness to embrace new things and in its rich endowment in creative ability, the Pacific Coast will move rapidly forward in programming services for its own viewers and in services that will span the continent just as so many of today's radio programs originate from the Hollywood-Los Angeles area," said Frank Stanton, president of CBS, and the president of the local Chamber of Commerce predicted that television would soon "take its place as a major influence on the economy of Los Angeles."

"I doubt that my grandson's children will have a sightless radio set in their home," Cecil B. DeMille prophesied.

As the decade drew to a close, so many Americans were sitting at home watching old movies on television, that weekly attendance at the country's motion picture houses had dropped from 90,000,000 to 46,000,000. But once a new film caught on it could return a profit ten to fifteen times greater than a hit picture in the days before television. "The future will lie in the big film," producers were saying. "Hollywood can't afford to make average pictures any more for theater showing. They can't compete with free TV."

A Russian film fan let the State Department know that moviemaking in Los Angeles was high on the list of things he wanted to have a look at when he visited the United States in the late summer of 1959.

"It is significant that Mr. Khrushchev should want to go to a film studio, as almost every non-Communist foreign visitor does, for he confesses, along with all the others, that Los Angeles' movies are one of the world's pervasive influences," the *Times* observed. In an earlier editorial, the paper had dismissed the notion that Communism and capitalism could ever live in peace. "Cold or hot, it will always be war," the editors felt, and they reminded their readers of Khrushchev's celebrated remark that the industrial production of his Socialist society would "bury" capitalism.

The Soviet Union's premier came calling at a time when his

country was well ahead of the United States in the exploration of outer space. "I see no reason for thinking of it merely as a competition with someone else," President Eisenhower said, but "a distinguished American scientist" told the Associated Press, "The Russians are driving toward manned flight to the moon and the planets. We had better be there when they arrive."

Mayor Poulson was waiting at Los Angeles International Airport with flowers for Mrs. Khrushchev when she and her sixty-five-year-old husband landed shortly after noon, September 19.

"Welcome to Los Angeles, the city of the angels, where the impossible always happens," the Mayor said, and whisked the city's Communist guests off to Twentieth Century Fox's capitalist commissary.

Nina Petrova Khrushchev, wearing a black suit and a white blouse, was seated between Bob Hope and Frank Sinatra, while her husband broke bread with the studio brass. "A darling, charming woman," Sinatra said of the shy, pleasant matron who stared at the stars around her and chatted in "excellent" English about his children and her grandchildren. She brought out snapshots and then, turning to Hope, she said, "I want to go to Disneyland." It was impossible to make the necessary security arrangements, she was told.

"She sent a note up to her husband," Hope explained later, "and that started the whole thing."

The crafty Russian peasant seized the opportunity to needle his well-heeled hosts by picturing himself as the innocent victim of American repression. "I thought I could come here as a free man," he said, and asked why the gates of Disneyland had been closed against him. "Is there some kind of cholera or launching pad out there? Have gangsters taken over the place?" He was politely shunted off to the San Fernando Valley to see a couple of model housing developments.

When a thousand or so Angelinos crowded into the Ambassador Hotel's Embassy Room that night, Khrushchev's host took advantage of the occasion to set forth his personal foreign policy.

"We do not agree with your widely quoted phrase, 'We shall bury you,'" Mayor Poulson said. "You shall not bury us and we shall not bury you."

Khrushchev, annoyed by this backcountry official who, he was heard to comment, "does not shine by his intelligence," said he was tired of having his remark quoted out of context. As he had explained time and again to the American press, he continued, he had never suggested that Communism would literally "bury" capitalism but that it would surpass and outlast it.

"Don't you read your own newspapers?" he asked. "In Russia, a provincial mayor would not be re-elected if he didn't keep up on the news."

Poulson's confrontaton with Khrushchev brought in 3,600 letters, he recalled in his memoirs, and they ran 3-1 in his favor. When he lost his 1961 reelection, it was due not to any lack of knowledge of current events but to his failure to provide his smog-plagued constituents a public transportation system capable of getting them around the metropolitan area with the ease their parents had enjoyed when riding Mr. Huntington's big red cars.

Sen. Robert F. Kennedy touches some of the many hands reaching out to him during a visit to the Plaza.

Chapter 9

Divide and Conquer
1960-1969

"We can end the divisions within the United States."

—ROBERT F. KENNEDY,
Ambassador Hotel, June 4, 1968

ON THE EVE of the 1960s a seven-pound monkey took off from Wallops Island, Virginia, strapped into a bell-shaped Mercury capsule and, after soaring to a height of fifty-five miles, splashed down safely in the Atlantic Ocean. Sometime in the new year an American astronaut was expected to replace the monkey on the capsule's contour couch and venture into the edges of space. In another year, perhaps, a man would be rocketed into orbit. On New Year's Day, 1960, it looked as though he would be a Russian.

A dark planetary cloud hung over the new decade, Blanca Holmes warned readers of Hedda Hopper's column. "Whenever Saturn conjuncts with Jupiter in Capricorn, an earth sign, it has a strong influence in world affairs," she said, and went on to explain that in astrological circles it was axiomatic that "no President going into office under the shadow of this conjunction . . . ever lives through his elected term of office."

Next day Senator John F. Kennedy announced his decision to seek the Democratic Party's nomination for President. He flew to Los Angeles in July to claim the victory he had won in the primaries of Wisconsin and West Virginia. The convention got off to an unfortunate start when the chairman of the committee that had selected Los Angeles was met at International Airport by two lawmen who tossed him in the Venice drunk tank. Then a workman at the Sports Arena discovered that the four caucus rooms under the podium had been bugged.

Delegates complained about the risks they ran in driving the city's freeways and the fares they paid to travel by cab. It cost a Pennsylvanian, sheltered in Pasadena, $15 to ride over to the midtown Los Angeles digs assigned to New Yorkers. But the natives were friendly and the relentless torrents of rhetoric were relieved by the sight of Golden Girls nipping about the Sports Arena in candystriped dresses. The convention turned out to be the most abstemious in the party's history. When the last cliche had sounded, janitors tidied up the place and found only ten empty whisky bottles.

* * *

On April 12, 1961, a month after John Kennedy moved into the White House (he was surprised to find "things were just as bad as we had been saying they were"), Russian Cosmonaut Yuri Gagarin completed an orbital flight around the earth in less than two hours. The young President spent much of a winter day the following year absorbed in the television coverage of John Glenn's five hour, three-orbital voyage on what Kennedy called this "new ocean." The United States, he said, had got off to a late start, but it would end up "the world's leading spacefaring nation."

Seven years later Colonel Glenn was in Los Angeles with the dead President's brother, Robert, when California Democrats went to the polls on June 4 to express their preference for a presidental candidate. California, Kennedy noted, "contains all the diverse elements of the national electorate." Its 1968 primary would present "a fair test" of each candidate's qualifications. Having just lost to Gene McCarthy in Oregon, the forty-two-year-old New York Senator had to win in California. If he didn't he intended to drop out of the race.

On election night Diane Broughton (pronounced *Brow*-ton), a twenty-three-year old Occidental College graduate, was in Bungalow Three of the Beverly Hills Hotel, keeping an eye on the six Kennedy children. Twelve-year-old David, she found, was "extremely bright, with a sharp, cool wit." Michael, age ten, struck her as "quiet, patiently polite, gentlemanly." Christopher, at four, was "charmingly gregarious and spontaneous," but his brother, Max, one year younger, seemed to be "leery of strangers." Courtney, at eleven, was "old for her years, witty, reserved, sensible, impatient." Her eight-year-old sister, Kerry, was "eager, erratic, volatile and unpredictable."

After dinner, when the four older children left to meet their parents at campaign headquarters in the Ambassador Hotel, Chris and Max were treated to chocolate sundaes. Diane overheard their theological discussion as to who was boss, God or Daddy. Chris won the argument, "God made Daddy and Daddy does what God wants, so that means God is boss."

The two young Kennedys were asleep when their brothers and sisters got back from Ambassador about 10:30. They were pleased to find Bob Galland, their twenty-one-year-old traveling companion, had managed to retrieve their spider monkey, Dr. Spock, from the tree where it had taken refuge from Kennedy roughhousing earlier in the day. Michael and the two girls went to their rooms, leaving David with Diane and Bob, who were watching the television coverage of the election returns. David was the only one of the children who stayed up to hear their father deliver his victory speech shortly after midnight.

"I think that we can end the divisions within the United States," he said.

When he finished speaking, Diane, David and Bob went back to talking politics until, she wrote in *West* Magazine (June 4, 1972) "we heard the TV newsmen yelling that someone had been hurt. My stomach gripped and I swooped down on the set to turn the volume up." David watched quietly, trembling at times, but saying nothing. Diane ripped a blanket from her bed and put it around him. Finally, when it became unbearable for the boy, Bob checked him into a first-floor room. Diane spent a sleepless night in the bungalow with Dr. Spock resting in the hollow of her throat.

Next morning, at their mother's request, Colonel Glenn came to the hotel to tell the children what had happened. "Last night a man shot your dad," he said. "He's in the hospital and it looks pretty bad." There were no tears, no emotional outbursts, Diane recalled. "It was as if they had been prepared for it."

Later that morning, while the children's things were being packed, their spider monkey escaped. Young Kennedys were in hot pursuit, waving sheets and blankets, when their mother called from Good Samaritan Hospital. Kerry told her about Dr. Spock. Once he had been captured and caged, the bungalow was quiet again. It was Courtney who broke the silence.

"Did Daddy win the election?" she asked bitterly, and Diane, matching her mood, said, "Yes, he won a big victory."

* * *

Angelinos in the sixties survived landslides in Brentwood and a devastating fire in Bel-Air, an incursion of the Beatles ("I like 'em because my parents hate 'em," a teenage idolater explained when asked what she saw in the four Liverpool mopheads), the introduction of the zip code, the disappearance of the Big Red Cars,

State Superintendent of Public Instruction Max Rafferty's effort to do away with dirty books ("The test for a dirty book is whether it can be read over radio and television or be printed in a newspaper") and Walter O'Malley's effort to get out of a $250,000 increase in the tax on his new Chavez Ravine stadium ("The Los Angeles Dodgers lost their Tax Series to Los Angeles County," the *New York Times* reported).

Although right-wing Southern Californians were busy attacking welfare payments, foreign aid, academic freedom, the United Nations, fluoridation of drinking water and the widespread distribution of polio vaccine (a Communist scheme to bring about socialized medicine), Bruce Bliven assured readers of *The Reporter* in 1962 that crackpots represented only a small minority of the population. "In fact," he wrote, "it may be in large measure because most people in California are typically American that so many fads originating there go on to sweep the nation."

"Oh my goodness," eighty-five-year-old Upton Sinclair exclaimed in the summer of 1964, when a reporter showed up at his door in Monrovia and asked him about President Johnson's war on poverty, "I've been warring on poverty since, I guess, I was about four years old." He identified himself as a socialist Democrat, and went on to explain, "What we want to do is bring into our industrial world the same democratic system we have in our government."

Angelinos got a more democratic system of state government when Chief Justice Earl Warren spoke for a majority of the Supreme Court in *Reynolds* v. *Sims* (1964), which forced a "one-man, one-vote" reapportionment of the California legislature. Before the decision, Los Angeles County, with a population of six million in the 1960 census had only one state senator. When the urbanized legislature met for the first time in January, 1967, the eight Southern California counties had twenty-two of the forty senate seats and forty-six of the eighty assembly seats.

"All of my fears have come true," said Senator Stephen P. Teale, a veteran rural lawmaker, when his fellow-senators were asked to state their committee preferences and more than half opted for Education. Only eight wanted Agriculture.

"This is a historic day," Mrs. Norman Chandler said on November 3, 1960, when the Board of Supervisors unanimously adopted a proposal to raise funds from private sources to help build a Music Center on Bunker Hill. Four years later, when the 3,250-seat Dorothy Chandler Pavilion opened its doors, *Time* magazine saw it as a "symbol of the steady upsurge of interest in matters cultural in a city that has felt itself too long dismissed as an uncouth poor relation of San Francisco." The Ahmanson Theater (2,100 seats) and the Mark Taper Form (750 seats) made their debut in the spring of 1967.

"Perhaps no one," David Halberstam wrote in *The Powers That Be*, "had as much to do with the changing of Los Angeles from a provincial hidebound community to a modern, somewhat more sophisticated and infinitely more tolerant modern *city* (it had always in the past been a very large, sprawling small town), from changing the *Los Angeles Times* from a reactionary provincial paper to a modern national one, than Dorothy Chandler."

Administratively, the change in the paper came about in April, 1960, when her thirty-two-year-old son, Otis, took over as publisher. Editorially, the change became apparent the following year, when the *Times* ran a series of articles on the John Birch Society which served notice on the community (and on the young publisher's Bircher uncle and aunt, Philip and Alberta Chandler) that a new generation was now in command at First and Spring Streets. If there were any doubts at the California Club, they were dispelled during the 1964 presidential campaign when the editorial page bristled with the political cartoons of Paul Conrad.

The tall, lean, owlish Iowan not only showed Barry Goldwater no mercy, he also gave the hallowed features of Dwight Eisenhower a look of cheerful idiocy. When the debacle was over, Conrad came up with a cartoon labelled "The Caretaker," which depicted an exhausted elephant sprawled on a cactus-dotted desert in Goldwater country, with a vulture perched on its rump. The vulture had the face of Richard Nixon who, at that time, was a friend of Conrad's employers.

Nixon ran up against the new order of things at the *Times* during his 1962 campaign to unseat Governor Pat Brown. For the first time in its history the paper gave fair and equal coverage to both the Democratic and Republican candidates, even measuring the amount of space the two men got each day. The policy change was brought home to Nixon by a confrontation with Dick Bergholz, a political reporter who had moved over from the defunct *Mirror*.

"Early in the campaign," says Halberstam, "Nixon called a group of reporters together and said he wanted to give them a briefing on Brown's campaign, but not for attribution, and Bergholz had quickly said no, none of that, don't pull your Washington game on us, Dick, either we can use it or don't say it. Nixon was stunned—a reporter talking to him like that, particularly a reporter from the *Los Angeles Times*."

The morning after his defeat Nixon met with reporters at the Beverly Hilton Hotel and delivered a fifteen-minute farewell address to the press corps remembered for one line, "You won't have Nixon to kick around any more, because, gentlemen, this is my last press conference." The rambling, revealing monologue included a passing attack on the "woolly heads" around President Kennedy "who want him to admit Red China to the U.N."

* * *

"Los Angeles is sweeping into high gear this year on a $101,179,805 expansion of the Civic Center," Ray Zeman reported in the *Times* as the 1960s opened, and rattled off a list of new public buildings designed to shelter peace officers, judges, law librarians, public health officials and a mind-curdling assortment of city, county, state and federal bureaucrats. Meanwhile, the Civic Center was being ringed by freeways. "Its northwest corner—Sunset Boulevard and Figueroa Street—will be a four-level cloverleaf and already ranks as the busiest automobile intersection in the world."

"We cannot build enough expressways to handle traffic in a

growing city," warned Congressman Charles L. Weltner of Atlanta, Georgia, in 1964. "There is a type of Parkinson's Law working here. 'One more lane of expressway will produce twice as many cars as it can handle.' "

Weltner had introduced a bill to provide federal funds to help cities "develop alternatives to expressways, traffic jams, parking lots and carbon monoxide," but nine years and three Presidents later, when Angelinos were still driving to work in their individual smog factories, the Secretary of Transportation reminded them that although federal money was available in his department for cities to plan and build rapid transit systems, none of it seemed to be going to Los Angeles.

"I have not seen an application yet," he said, dismayed by the sight of so many millions of automobile addicts who "don't know how to break the habit."

When Caskie Stinnett, *Holiday Magazine's* graceful stylist, spotted a 1963 news story on the opening of a Los Angeles "walk-in mental health center," he predicted it would not "long remain a walk-in service. It's going to be drive-in, and the patient will get a mental toning up without turning off his ignition. It's not beyond possibility that a car-wash be operated in conjunction with the enterprise."

Angelinos roared with rage and pain in the summer of 1961 when a Las Vegas civil defense official disclosed plans for a 5,000-man militia to repulse Southern Californians who, in the event of a thermonuclear attack, could be expected to "come in like a swarm of human locusts, and pick the valley clean of food, medical supplies and other goods."

While Nevada officials were taking steps to defend the state's resources against a wartime invasion of its neighbors, a parcel of private citizens on the other side of the border, alarmed by the daily influx of 1,600 new Californians, was trying to awaken public officials to the need to husband the state's resources. These peacetime locusts were swarming over a deteriorating paradise dotted with what the founding fathers of California Tomorrow called "slurbs," a word they defined as "sloppy, sleazy, slovenly, slipshod semi-cities."

"We might have to decide how big a given city should be, in order to sponsor healthy home life, healthy business and industry while protecting agriculture and the beauty of our countryside," the group declared, and Assembly Speaker Jesse Unruh of Los Angeles agreed that "we run the real risk of turning bright and golden California into a smog-ridden, sprawling wasteland of a parking lot, unfit for human habitation and useless to agriculture."

From his office at Twentieth Century Fox Film Corporation ("Here I am, back in the Industry for a spell, but thinking of another historical study for later on"), Aldous Huxley dropped a note to his bookseller friend, Jake Zeitlin, asking for some books relating to "the case of the diabolic possessions at Loudun, during the seventeenth century." In an aside, he conveyed his gratitude to Mrs. Zeitlin for having sent him a copy of a book he mistakenly referred to as *Prelude to a Master Plan*.

"I suppose the trouble will be that the prelude is not likely at any near date to be followed by the plan, and that while they're thinking about it, Los Angeles will grow out of all recognition and the problem become even more difficult and costly to solve than it is at present," Huxley wrote in the erroneous belief that the book had just come out. Actually, twenty years had gone by since publication of *Los Angeles: Preface to a Master Plan*, edited by George W. Robbins and L. Deming Tilton.

Clarence Dykstra, in the book's introductory essay, had referred to Los Angeles as a boastful, adolescent city which, because of "its size, rapid growth, and the serious nature of its problems," should recognize the compelling need for "a vigorous, well-supported comprehensive study of its future, it prospects, its potentialities, its limitations, and organic problems."

California, the Census Bureau calculated, would overtake New York and become the country's most populous state on July 1, 1964, but Governor Brown, using the projections of his own population experts, insisted the historic event had taken place sometime in the fall of 1962. He called on his constituents to join him in a four-day celebration.

"As the momentous shift of population from the Atlantic to the Pacific has come about, we have met it with the vision and determination characteristic of our people," he proclaimed on October 15, 1962.

It would have been a proud and glorious day for General Otis, but his great-grandson's editors, whose children were attending half-day sessions and turning up with respiratory ailments, were having second thoughts about the booster spirit which had deposited more than 6,000,000 people in Los Angeles County.

"The promise and potential of bigness can be lost if the problems it creates are ignored," the paper editorialized, and featured a sobering article by Paul Weeks: "Rampant growth breeds crises that take up permanent abode—traffic strangulation, water shortage, air pollution, school overcrowding, racial pressures, exploding slums, rising crime, overloaded court calendars, overtaxed recreational facilities, fire and flood peril, hospital bed shortages, disrupted family ties in a rootless population."

"After twenty-five years of haphazard growth and unprecedented prosperity, Los Angeles now faces the same tough economic and social problems that confronted older cities years ago," the editors of *U.S. News & World Report* concluded in the summer of 1965, when the flames of Watts made it clear for all to see that "the easy life is coming to an end in the country's third largest city."

* * *

On the hot summer night of Wednesday, August 11, 1965, two black youths driving home in their mother's ten year old Buick were stopped around 7 o'clock by a white California Highway Patrol officer on Avalon Boulevard, just north of 116th Place. A crowd gathered, the officer broadcast a Code 1199 ("Officer Needs Help!") and, after a bit of scuffling and name-calling, the lawmen drove off with the two young men, their mother and a black girl who had come out of a nearby beauty parlor, hair still in curlers, to see what was going on.

The Watts-Willowbrook area exploded. After six days of burning and looting, 34 persons were dead, 1,032 wounded, and 3,952 had been arrested. Property damage was estimated at $40,000,000. In the flames of Charcoal Alley, white Angelinos caught a glimpse of the pent-up anger and frustration of rural blacks trapped in an urban slum patrolled by white police officers long on zeal and short on sensitivity.

Police Chief William H. Parker bridled at any suggestion that the riot (or, as they called it in Watts, the uprising) had sprung from smoldering resentment of police brutality. Quite the contrary, he insisted, the trouble might never have happened if the police had not been handling Negroes "with kid gloves." The eruption should be attributed to the weather, he insisted. People had simply given vent to their emotions on an uncomfortably warm evening.

"I'd be out of sorts now," the chief told reporters, "if I didn't have air conditioning."

Blacks in Los Angeles had been making do not only without air conditioning, but also without jobs, education, decent housing, adequate medical care, parks and public transportation. Ten years after the embers of Watts had cooled, the community had a $39 million hospital, the city had a black mayor and the state a black lieutenant governor, but the unemployment rate for young blacks was still more than forty percent.

"The majority of people are worse off today than they were in '65," Bishop H. H. Brookins of the African Methodist Episcopal Church said in the spring of 1975, and Police Chief Ed Davis agreed. "There's a state of despair with a lot of people. In almost any way of measuring, things are worse than they were ten years ago."

* * *

When the country's governors assembled at Minoru Yamasaki's handsome, gently curving Century Plaza Hotel in the summer of 1966 for their fifty-eighth annual conference, it looked as though George Romney of Michigan would be the Republican chosen to run against Lyndon Johnson in 1968, but Robert E. Smylie of Idaho thought California's actor-candidate, Ronald Reagan, would take the Governor's Mansion away from the Brown family and start aiming at the White House. Within a year Republicans around the country where cheerfully shelling out $100 to break bread with Governor Reagan.

"If we don't win the next election, $100 is likely to become the *regular* price of a dinner," he would say at the start of his standard speech.

Gladwin Hill, who heard it time and again while covering California for the *New York Times,* describes it in *Dancing Bear* as carefully crafted to convey the impression "that Reagan was the warm, entertaining fellow of screen roles, now turned unassuming but earnest statesman; that he was a dedicated foe of undue governmental power and extravagance; and that he had implanted a remarkable common-sense citizen's approach to government of California, with particular attention to economy. Capping all this was an unabashed flag-waving finish bespeaking Republican unity and equating the party's future with the welfare not only of the nation but all the world."

While their parents dined with Ronnie and Nancy, runaway teenagers converged on the land of the hot rod and the ninth wave, turning the Sunset Strip into the night club capital of their restless, pot-smoking, acid-tripping generation. Dinner jackets and mink coats gave way to leather jackets and stretch pants as the Flower Children writhed to the Watusi and the Mashed Potato on this mile-long stretch of county territory where the stars of the first talking pictures had guzzled bootleg scotch.

"It's where the action is," a young fugitive from Chicago told *Newsweek* in 1966, and out in the San Fernando Valley, the heartland of family, flag and church, a sixteen-year-old high school girl told a reporter, "sometimes when I'm sitting in my room I just feel like screaming and pounding my pillow. I'm so confused about the whole world and everything that's happening. My friends just sit back and say, 'Wow, it's happening.'"

Leonard Alfred Schneider, renamed Lenny Bruce, died on a bathroom floor of his house above the Strip on the night of August 3, 1966, a hypodermic needle in his right arm. Within two years a cult had sprung up around the night-club messiah known to his young disciples only through his writings and his records. They had never sat at his feet, never touched the hem of his garment, but they cherished his message, "Every day people are straying away from the church and going back to God."

In a pious community where the Yellow Pages listed such organizations as Air Mail From God Mission, Full Gospel Business Men's Fellowship, Sky Pilot Radio Church and Christ for Greater Los Angeles, it was hardly surprising that Hollywood's two-drink-minimum tabernacles had produced a new prophet who delivered his parables in a scatological jargon capable of blistering paint.

American evangelists have never shown much respect for the fancy jargon of divinity schools. In the early days of the Republic, when circuit riders were carrying the oldtime religion to backwoods heathen, they translated Yale theology into the plain linsey-woolsey terms of the frontier. They preached a no-nonsense brand of damnation and salvation. You could come to Christ or go to hell.

At the turn of the century, when Billy Sunday left the Chicago White-stockings outfield to trumpet the call to temperance and ever-lasting life, he spoke the earthy corn-belt idiom he knew best. "I like good old Anglo-Saxon words," he said, and, replying to critics of his coarse, comical style, he quoted Charles Grandison Finney, the early nineteenth-century evangelist who had answered similar objections by saying, "God Almighty may use any method or means or individual that he pleases in order to promote a revival."

The *Indianapolis Star*, in its obituary, identified Lenny Bruce as "one of the minor gods of the widespread and largely incoherent revolution of the dissatisfied and 'alienated' generation that is still trying to make a religion out of drugs, sex, pacifism, four-letter words and kicking apart what it considers the outworn remnants of the civilizations that came before it." A revolutionary effort to promote peace had been made two thousand years ago, Indiana Congressman Andrew Jacobs, Jr., pointed out and, he added, "some of the dissatisfied are still trying."

Lenny was resurrected by young rebels at a time when their middle-aged parents had grown accustomed to watching a war in living color on a nineteen-inch screen during the cocktail hour. Small children were free to wander in and out of the room while Asian huts were going up in flames and American soldiers were being blown to bits between beer commercials, but the youngsters would have been sent away if they had drifted in while two people were taking off their clothes and climbing into bed. To Lenny's pacificist flock, the ultimate obscenity was war, not love.

* * *

Young idealists who had gone to Alabama to join the Freedom Riders and to New Hampshire to take part in the Gene McCarthy Children's Crusade swarmed over Hollywood on the night of May 27, 1969, heading for the Palladium, where they looked forward to sharing the victory of their new mayor, Tom Bradley, the first black in the city's history to mount a major campaign for the office.

In the April 1 primary three out of four voters had rejected Sam Yorty, the incumbent, whose administration had been marked by dissension, absenteeism, scandal (four of his commissioners had resigned under fire, five had been indicted) and a refusal to reply to Bradley's demand for an accounting of the $700,000 he had collected over the years at birthday dinners.

"I haven't let loose on him yet," Yorty told reporters when Bradley took the primary by a hundred thousand votes.

In the final weeks of the runoffs, the mayor bore down heavily on Bradley's "racial coalition of left-wingers." Yorty backers drove around white neighborhoods with bumper stickers showing a clenched black fist against a red background. They bore the label: BRADLEY POWER. Despite implied threats of black gangs prowling the streets of the San Fernando Valley, while their red allies in City Hall did away with the free enterprise system, Bradley had 53 percent of the vote in an election-eve poll. When the final returns were in, however, it was Sam Yorty, not Tom Bradley, who had the 53 percent.

"He has retained his office as the result of the most desperate, divisive campaign ever waged in this city," the *Times* declared, and *The New Republic* found the result "frightening," because "it shows what can be done by an unscrupulous candidate who sets out to put people in fear of their lives."

Leon H. Washington, publisher of the city's influential black newspaper, the *Sentinel*, praised Bradley for having waged "a beautiful campaign." "An elegant man," said the editors of *The Nation* and called attention to the large number of young Angelinos among the bitterly disappointed supporters who waited at the Palladium until nearly two o'clock in the morning to hear their candidate's concession of defeat.

"We have tried to prove that the democratic process can work," Bradley told them. "Never give up that hope. I have lived by that belief all my life, and I will not give up now. This city, this nation, does not begin or end with one man. Keep faith with what we are trying to do. We have put together a coalition of conscience and concern. We have just begun our journey together. Go home now in an orderly fashion."

Tom Bradley, UCLA's top quarter-miler in the late 1930s, still remembers his best time: forty-eight seconds.

Chapter 10

Present Indicative
1970 – 1980

"Dream big dreams."
—TOM BRADLEY, 1974

THE MORNING after white voters made it clear they were not ready to deliver City Hall to a black mayor, Tom Bradley launched a new drive to restore Sam Yorty to private life.

"I grew up under the system that said "you can't do this, you can't go there, you cannot achieve this position," he said when he took his second campaign to the Los Angeles campus of the University of California, where he had graduated in the Class of 1940.

In junior high school a teacher had told him to study something practical so "you can get a job, because you'll never go beyond high school if you're lucky enough to finish." After UCLA, he had gone to work for the predominantly white Los Angeles Police Department (black officers were assigned to either a black community or to downtown traffic), studied law at night and in 1963 had become the first black Angelino to conduct a successful campaign for a seat on the City Council.

Ten years later, in his second race for mayor, when the polls put him ahead of Yorty by 6 percentage points on the eve of the May 29 runoff, the Mayor's campaign strategists sent a terse telegraphic message to several hundred thousand households in white precincts. In the April 3 primary, which Bradley had won, the turnout was low, the white voters were reminded and then they were told: "Watts had a phenomenally high turnout. Black bloc vote went massively for Bradley. Radical elements could control our police department and city services, as in Berkeley."

On election night Bradley was watching television in a sixteenth floor suite of the Los Angeles Hilton when, an hour after the polls closed, he was told that NBC had predicted his victory.

"I'd rather wait until they count a few more votes before I get too excited," he said, and continued watching an episode of the CBS comedy series, *Maude*. He broke out laughing when one of the characters, speaking to a black maid, described domestic work as the kind of job white people gave to black people because white people didn't want to do it themselves.

"Yeah, yeah," Bradley chortled, "like being mayor of Los Angeles."

A few hours later, the fifty-five-year old mayor-elect, whose mother had supported her five children by working as a domestic, got a chance to make use of the victory address he had hoped to deliver four years earlier.

"Tonight was the fulfillment of a dream, the impossible dream," he said, and went on to point out that, with the ending of the era of unrestricted growth, the city would have to pay more attention to the quality of life. For openers, he promised to get cracking on a rail rapid transit system.

In an extemporaneous talk to youngsters in a black school a year later, the Mayor recalled the days when he was "where you are now. There wasn't much hope for me or the others who went to Twentieth Street Elementary School then, but there's a great deal of opportunity for all of you now. The only thing that can stop you is you. Dream big dreams, work hard, study hard and listen to your teachers. Above all, get along with each other. You can be anything your heart wants you to be."

* * *

The Class of 1979, as first-graders, had come home one unforgettable fall day in 1963 to find their parents transfixed before their television sets, as President Lyndon Johnson flew back to Washington with the body of John Kennedy. During the next sixteen years they watched their older brothers march off to Vietnam or slip across the border to Canada, while their older sisters went on the Pill and their parents shuddered at a world teeming with an alienated, drug-crazed, foul-tongued, free-loving generation of disbelievers who trusted no one over thirty.

For young rebels of the counterculture, the 1960s ended in bloodshed at Kent State on May 4, 1970. For their parents, children of the New Deal, the decade of protest and confrontation came to an end on June 16, 1978 when a gruff, belligerent, seventy-five-year-old Angelino named Howard Jarvis touched off a nation-wide tax revolt of a seismic magnitude comparable to the Depression which spawned Big Government.

"The only way to cut government spending is not to give them the money in the first place," he had been saying for years before he teamed up with Paul Gann, a sixty-five-year-old legislator, to draft a ballot initiative designed to redraw the borders of Big Government by calling for an amendment (Proposition 13) to the state constitution slashing property taxes and limiting their future growth.

Proposition 13 hit the national fan at a time when inflation had cut the value of the dollar 47.6 percent in a little more than ten years. To make matters worse, the property tax on the homeowner's $40,000 bungalow, now assessed at $80,000, had gone up to $2,800 a year. Under Jarvis-Gann, it would drop to around $1,200. Without Jarvis-Gann, it would keep on climbing. Lawmakers in Sacramento could not be counted on to make any substantial reduction in property taxes, which, thanks to inflation, gave them a steadily rising source of revenue without subjecting them to the politically hazardous process of voting for a tax increase.

"The tax became a bureaucratic dream," Phil Kerby later wrote in the *Times*. "Rivers of cash flowed into Sacramento, and the state accumulated a massive surplus, yet a year before Howard Jarvis appeared on the scene, the legislature defeated a meek attempt to return a mere one-tenth of this vast fund to homeowners."

Young couples with incomes of $30,000 a year could not afford to buy a house in Los Angeles at the close of the 1970s, when Richard Reeves looked into the housing market for *The New Yorker* (December, 24, 1979). The head of a department at UCLA, he wrote, told him "that he sought out homosexuals when recruiting new instructors, because 'people with families can't afford to come here anymore, and gays are willing to live in tiny apartments in West Hollywood.' "

Fred Case, a UCLA professor of urban-land economics, showed Reeves a single-family home price index plotted on graph paper. "The curve of the index looks like half of a postcard photograph of the Eiffel Tower," Reeves reported. "There is a more or less flat line, like the ground, from 1900 to 1940, a period in which the index began at $2,000 and rose, almost imperceptibly, to $4,500. From 1940 to 1973, the line approximates the base of the tower, rising from that $4,500 to $37,000. In 1973, the line begins to shoot almost straight up, rising in five years from $37,000 to $105,000—an average annual rate of increase of about thirty-seven percent."

"There is an unspoken conspiracy among suppliers, builders, real-estate people, and government to drive the prices up," Case explained. "They all benefit from higher housing prices, and there's no resistance on the demand side to stop it . . . If there were seventeen percent inflation, some people wouldn't be able to buy things like clothing, and they might start saying, 'It's this damned house.' There could be more houses going on the market, for a while, then there would be buyers. There would at least be a slower turnover. But I have to admit I've been saying that for a long time, and even my students have been going out and making money in this thing."

"Well, we're a *little* insane," a trim, business-like real estate agent admitted when she showed Richard C. Wald, a television network executive a $200,000 "fixer-upper" in Santa Monica, which consisted of a wood porch and a doorway, nothing more. "But," she pointed out, "it *is* Santa Monica."

As the 1980s began only fifteen percent of Los Angeles households earned more than $40,000 a year and it required an annual income of $50,000 or more to swing the monthly payments on a $115,000 home (the median price at the time). Kathleen Connell, head of the housing division of the city's Community Development Department, was convinced that "the housing crisis will be the issue in the eighties that the civil rights issue was in the sixties, because it will be hitting the average core of society—the middle-income person. I think we're going to see a revolution in this country on personal rights versus property rights."

* * *

After the turbulence of the "Hell, no, we won't go!" sixties, the smiling, jogging, self-indulgent "Have a nice day" seventies seem peaceful in retrospect, but along with the digital watches and the pet rocks, the Perrier water, discotheques, miniskirts and microwave ovens, it was a time of terrorist bombings and highjackings, the casting adrift of "the boat people," the coming to power of the Ayatollah Ruhollah Khomeni, the bloodshed at Attica prison, the slaughter of the innocents at Jonestown, the Charles Manson murders and the shootout that incinerated six members of the Symbionese Liberation Army but spared Patty Hearst.

It was also the period when a streaker broke in on the Academy Awards and truckers babbled a strange new jargon ("A big 10-four, good buddy"), when two Popes died and a born-again Baptist running for President rapped with *Playboy* ("I've committed adultery in my heart many times"), when Anwar Sadat visited Israel and Israelis swooped down on Entebbe, when Angelinos waited in line to get a tankful of gas or see *Star Wars*, when homosexuals came out of the closet and housewives came out of the kitchen, when mothers who worried in college about "going all the way" wondered how to introduce the neighbors to their son's "live-in."

"Women and men now talk about it openly," Michelle Triola said in 1980, a year after her suit against actor Lee Marvin led to a California Supreme Court ruling that permitted unmarried persons living together to claim property rights when the relationship ended.

Midway through the seventies, when CBS objected to having Maude Findlay call her husband a "son of a bitch," Norman Lear, creator of the *All in the Family* spinoff, invited the network executives to "come up with anything else that the audience would believe." They couldn't, and the historic epithet was hurled as written. Once the switchboards began to light up in Los Angeles and New York, Lear was pleased to learn that 70 percent of the calls were from women who said, "Thank God, I've wanted to say that to my husband so many times."

"We have come through the dark sixties craving humor, because humor reduces the threat of that which endangers us," said Chaytor Mason, a USC psychologist, and Kenneth S. Lynn, a Johns Hopkins University historian agreed. In the sixties, he pointed out, "we lost the power to criticize minority groups. But when the Archie Bunker program became one of the most popular on T.V., we found that through humor we could begin to get certain things off our chests, express our prejudices."

* * *

"If there's anything I would hope to see from the Bicentennial, it is the creation of a feeling of belonging to a city, by a large part of society that right now hardly knows it belongs to the city," Albert Martin, the chairman of the forty-four-member Los Angeles 200 Committee, said in the spring of 1980, when Angelinos were preparing to launch a year-long commemoration of the city's founding.

Two centuries after eleven families were recruited in Mexico to establish a Spanish colonial village in Alta California, the sprawling, polyglot American metropolis was overrun by upwards of half a million Mexicans who had sneaked across a friendly border and made their way north to the city's teeming barrios. Once the *illegales* started spilling over into South Central Los Angeles, middle-aged residents of the black community found themselves echoing the sentiments voiced by an earlier generation of Caucasions when Negro families first intruded on white neighborhoods.

"I been here more than twenty years," an elderly man told a *Times* reporter. "When I came here this was almost all blacks. Now there's only five black families on the block. The Mexicans, they coming in big droves. Goddang it, what gonna become of the people here?"

"These illegal aliens don't want to be told anything," said a woman in her fifties, who had lived in the neighborhood since 1957. "They say this is their country and they want it back. They're taking our jobs and our housing, and they're pushing the colored people out . . . I even had one who told me to go back to Africa."

When members of the Select Commission on Immigration and Refugee Policy, held hearings in Los Angeles in February, 1980, Wendell Green, vice chairman of a black organization called the Committee for Representative Government, told of black breadwinners whose jobs in the construction and garment industries had been taken over by Mexicans. An already tight housing market, he said, had been overwhelmed by undocumented workers who were welcomed by slum landlords because their fear of the authorities kept them from complaining about intolerable conditions.

"We have not spoken out before because we're extremely hesitant to become allies with bigots and racists," Green said, and made it clear he had no intention of playing "the power structure's game of divide and conquer."

"We're all in the same boat," said Anne Davis, a twenty-three-year-old black social worker, who liked to remind her elders that the poverty they shared with their new Mexican neighbors made them fellow victims' of economic exploitation. "When the hand comes down," she pointed out, "it comes down on all of us."

Ironically, both black Angelinos and their Chicano neighbors have long been segregated by whites in a city founded by black and brown colonists. Young Chicanos see reminders of their historic contributions to the Anglo metropolis in streets named for their forebears and in the tourist attraction city fathers have made of the Plaza, but black children are left in ignorance of their heritage. Few ever learn that the San Fernando Valley and Beverly Hills were once owned by blacks; that Pio Pico, the last of the Mexican governors of California, had a grandmother listed by census-takers as a *mulata*; and that one of the first two Americans to settle in Los Angeles was a black man named Thomas Fisher, who came ashore from a pirate ship in 1818.

In the years preceding the Civil War, a black barber, Peter Biggs, was much in evidence along Main Street, where he figured in a rich body of anecdote. Georgia-born Biddy Mason came to California as a slave in 1851, won her freedom in court, went to work for a white doctor, put her savings in real estate and built a home at 331 South Spring Street known to every Angelino down on his luck. The softest touch in town, Mrs. Mason once left word with a grocery store to give flood victims whatever they needed and put it on her tab.

On February 12, 1909, taking note of the one hundredth anniversary of Abraham Lincoln's birth, the *Times* published a supplement devoted to the city's black community. Its leading capitalist was Biddy Mason's grandson, Robert C. Owens, who, with his brother, Henry, had once run a stable on the family's Spring Street property. Like his grandmother, he had also dabbled in real estate. A lot on Hill Street between Seventh and Eighth, bought in 1890 for $7,200, had sold in 1905 for $75,000. As for the family's Spring Street property, the paper pointed out, it "could not be bought for a quarter of a million dollars."

Between 1910 and 1920 the number of black Angelinos more than doubled, jumping from 7,599 to 15,579, but they still made up only 2.7 percent of the city's total population. In the 1920s their ranks again doubled and the city's whites kept them isolated by housing covenants. They were permitted to swim in public pools only on Thursdays, the day before the water was changed.

In 1934, when blacks were competing with whites for non-existent jobs and the city was undergoing one of its intermittent Red scares, Chief of Police James E. Davis drove over to Pasadena to share his expertise on Communism with his colleagues at the annual convention of the state's peace officers.

"Here in Los Angeles," the chief said, "to practically demonstrate that under Communism pigmentation of skin makes no difference, quite a number of white Communist females are living with Negroes. And that is having a tremendous psychological effect among the blacks not alone of Los Angeles but throughout the nation, where that national program of living with Negroes is practiced by Communist girls. So that the twelve or fifteen million of those Negroes living in America can see that the last great prejudice retained by any people that are white against the blacks is that of living together, and that prejudice cannot exist under Communism. So that tremendous progress is being made with that racial group."

The number of black Angelinos rose in the 1930s from 38,894 to 63,744. By 1946 blacks represented 7.36 percent of the city's population. Horace R. Cayton, co-author of *Black Metropolis*, looked in on the postwar city and found it "overcrowded, tense and tawdry," but "most of the middle class and upper class Negroes, as well as a good number of just common folk, have purchased attractive private dwellings in nice, quiet neighborhoods." He was taken aback by the ardor with which white Angelinos enforced restrictive covenants ("they even use them against American Indians"), but, he reported in *Negro Digest* (October, 1947), "people up and down Central Avenue seem very happy . . . ."

During the 1950s the number of blacks in the city leaped from 171,209 to 334,916, but despite a 1948 Supreme Court decision outlawing racial covenants, whites had been so successful in keeping them out of their neighborhoods that in 1960 only 21,050 lived outside the city's central district. Even when families moved away, they were likely to end up in the black ghettos of San Pedro, Venice and Pacoima.

"This is the most segregated city I've ever known," said a black businessman from the South in 1962.

Back in 1904, when two black Angelinos went to court to protest discrimination by the Grand Opera House, their lawyer, F. W. Allender, suggested that the time had come "for the citizens of this city to settle the matter of which laws they will obey. If the Mississippi plan of having one law for white people and one for Negroes is to obtain, we should know it now. However, we do not believe public sentiment in this city will tolerate the heathenism practiced upon law-abiding Negroes in Mississippi and in other states."

Two generations later, when children went back to school at the start of the 1970-71 term, fifteen years had passed since the

Supreme Court's ruling against racially segregated schools, but while more than 26 percent of Mississippi's black children and nearly 45 percent of South Carolina's were attending predominantly white schools, only 6 percent of the 155,000 black schoolchildren of Los Angeles were going to school in the city's white enclaves.

Superior Court Judge Paul Egly ordered the Los Angeles Unified School District in the summer of 1977 to commence desegregation "realistically," but by the spring of 1980 minority children made up at least half of the student body in 427 of the district's 612 schools. In 217 schools there was at least 70 percent minority enrollment and in 149 schools the figure was 90 percent or more. In a single decade the percentage of white students in the school system had dropped from 50 to 27. By 1985, demographers predicted, it would be 15 percent.

"Segregated education is inherently unequal in a multi-cultural society and the damage done, especially to minority students, cannot be changed except through integration," a faculty committee of a black junior high school wrote Judge Egly when it began to look as though he might abandon the idea of total desegregation and, instead, throw more money at minority schools. "Money, services and facilities, no matter how excessive," the junior high teachers declared, "cannot, in our opinion adequately compensate for the values, feelings and experience which can be gained by the student in a truly integrated setting."

"Do you believe integration is an important goal?" Mayor Tom Bradley was asked on the eve of his sixty-first birthday in 1978.

"I think it is," he said. "I think that until people begin to interrelate with each other in a normal fashion, where it becomes a natural event for them, they're not going to have the values that can come from intercultural social change, not going to have full and mutual respect, one race to another. Until that happens, there will continue to be disparity in terms of opportunity, in terms of equality of treatment, job opportunity and all the rest."

* * *

Chicanos drop out of school a year or two earlier than their black contemporaries. Like the black children, they are born into a world where houses are falling apart, food is scarce, jobs hard to come by, streets ridden with crime and classrooms overcrowded, but the young Mexican-American runs up against the additional barrier of speaking a foreign language in the land of his ancestors.

"You know it from the beginning: speaking Spanish makes you different," Ruben Salazar wrote in *Stranger in One's Land*. "Your mother, father, brothers, sisters, and friends all speak Spanish. But the bus driver, the teacher, the policeman, the store clerk, the man who comes to collect the rent—all the people who are doing the important things—do not. Then the day comes when your teacher—who has taught you the importance of many things—tells you that speaking Spanish is wrong . . . ."

"The Chicano is completely lost in this society," Sydney Reibscheid of the *Los Angeles Daily Journal* was told in the summer of 1972 when she interviewed Legal Aid Community Representative Eduardo Ruiz. "Even though he lives in the American society, he is completely outside of it. He has Spanish television stations and Spanish stores. In reality, he doesn't even have to read the English language in order to get along. The only time he needs it is when he goes to buy a refrigerator or a television. And then if he only knows Spanish, he will be charged double price."

One out of four Angelinos had a Spanish surname at the close of the 1970s, but in city-wide elections they cast only about 5 percent of the votes. "People don't listen to us because they know we can't get back at them on election day," Deputy Mayor Grace Montanez Davis told a *Times* reporter in the fall of 1979. As a result, Hispanics found themselves without representation on the City Council or on the county Board of Supervisors. Statewide, although they accounted for more than 14,000,000 of California's population of 23,000,000, they had succeeded in electing only 8 of the 120 members of the legislature. In Washington, they had a lone Congressman.

For years the Spanish-speaking families of the Ninth Councilmanic District had been represented in City Hall by their political *Papacito*, Edward Roybal. When he was elected to Congress in 1962, the City Council was feuding with the Mayor, as usual, and to assert its independence, it took the seat away from a Chicano candidate in Yorty's office (he also happened to be a cousin of Roybal's) and gave it to Supervisor Kenneth Hahn's sixty-two-year-old black field deputy, Gilbert Lindsay.

In 1964, when councilmanic districts were redrawn to conform with the Supreme Court's reapportionment rulings, Councilman Lindsay got the downtown area, thus acquiring a pride of corporate constituents who have contributed generously to his re-election campaigns. In the meantime, two other blacks had been elected to the City Council. Their three seats were still held by blacks in 1980, but Boyle Heights Chicanos of the Fourteenth District were represented by an Anglo.

"Unlike the Negroes, the second largest minority in California, Mexican-Americans have no real political cohesion," Ruben Salazar pointed out in 1963, and cited a 1961 effort to incorporate East Los Angeles. Less than half of the barrio's voters (46 percent) had bothered to go to the polls. Incorporation lost by 340 votes.[*]

On August 29, 1970, five years after the Watts explosion, violence erupted in East Los Angeles, and one of its victims was Ruben Salazar who was killed by a tear gas missile fired into the Silver Dollar Cafe on Whittier Boulevard by a member of the Sheriff's department. A year later, community leaders agreed, the barrio still faced the same basic problems—unemployment, poor housing, inadequate educational opportunities, lack of political representation and strained relations with the police.

"I sometimes feel that out of the ashes just came more ashes," said Richard Martinez, president of the Congress of Mexican-American Unity.

---

* In 1974 it was rejected by 58 percent of the voters.

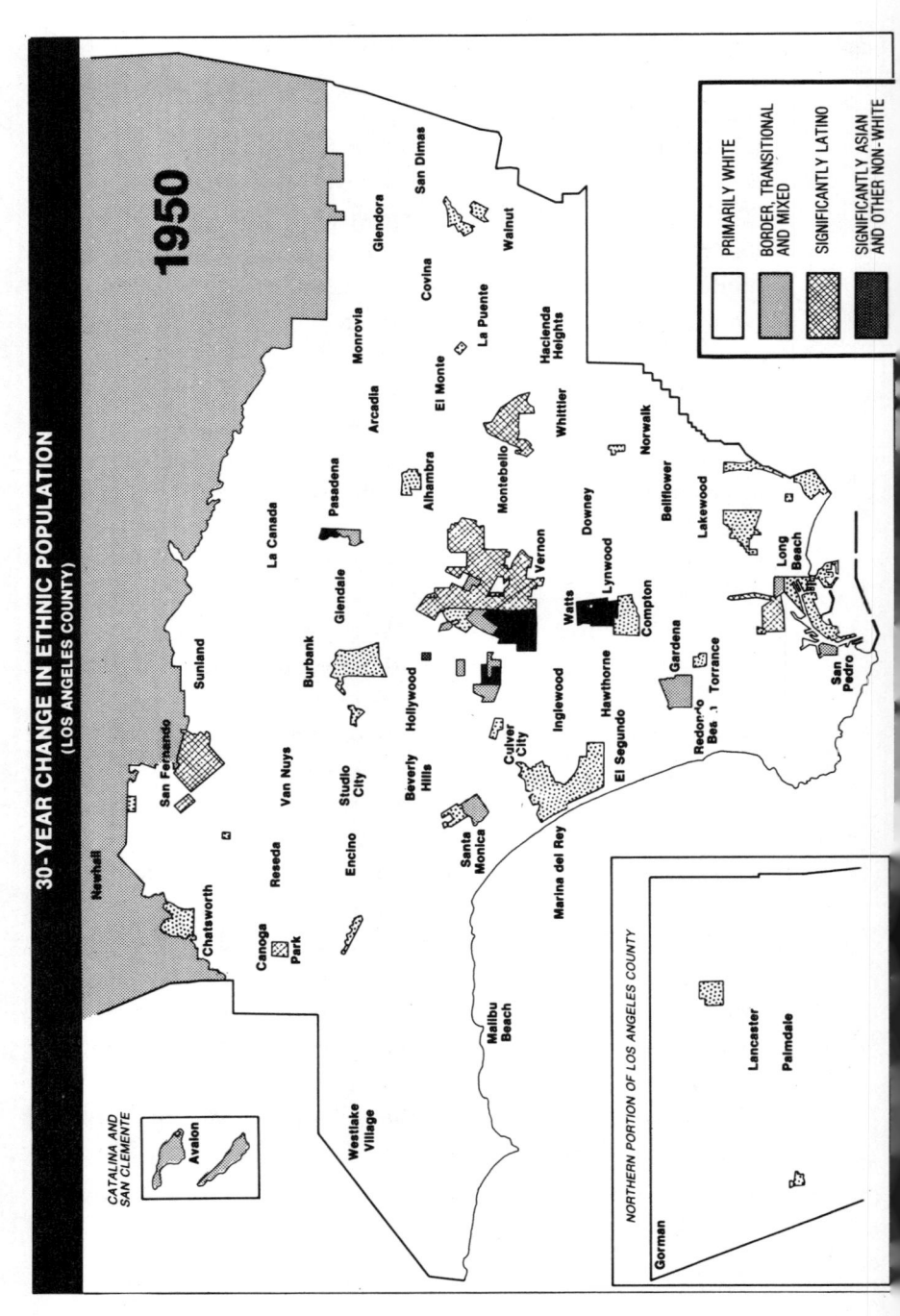

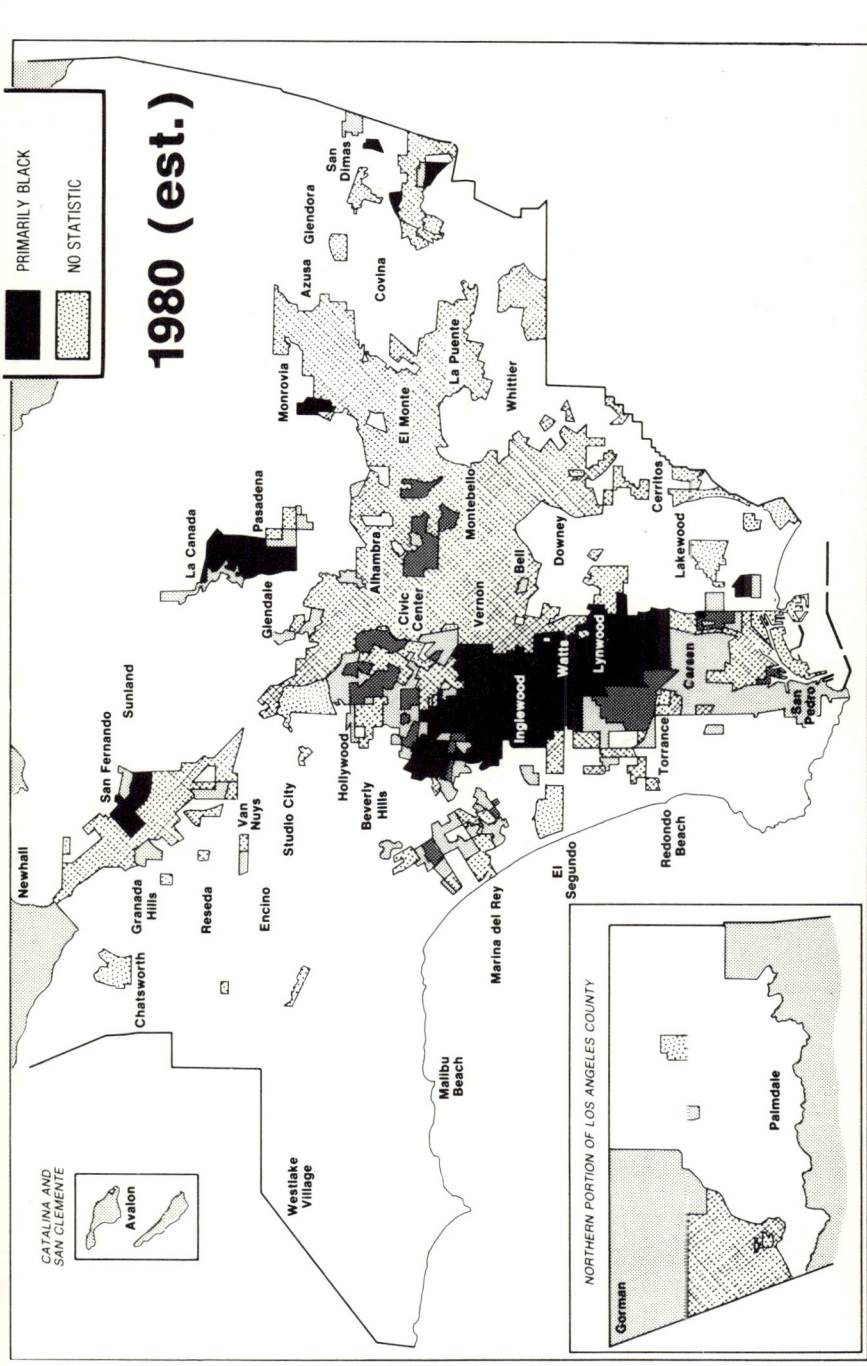

A CHANGING MOSAIC—*In 1950 Los Angeles was a white area, with Latinos making up only sizable minorities in some communities and blacks the majority just in Watts. Thirty years later, the minorities were on the verge of forming the majority.*

* * *

"We're fighting with the blacks and Chicanos for the same piece of pie," Irene Chu, a social worker with a master's degree from UCLA, said in 1978, speaking for a dissatisfied generation of young Chinese-Americans who wanted something more out of life than washing dishes, selling curios, making noodles and sewing piecework in garment factories. "We're called the quiet minority," Ms Chu added. "We don't scream as loud."

In the latter half of the 1970s an estimated 4,000 immigrants settled in Chinatown, the cultural center for some 150,000 Chinese-American Angelinos. Like the first Chinese who came to California in the mid-nineteenth century to mine gold and build railroads, they have been forced to make do with substandard shelter, low wages and long hours.

"We would certainly like to see, instead of more sewing factories, an electronics assembly plant," Robert Gee, president of the local Chinese Chamber of Commerce said in 1980, but for the immediate future he foresaw "more of the same damn thing—restaurants, gift shops...."

Chinese-American Angelinos rallied to the aid of the 60,000 Vietnamese, Laotians and Cambodians who found their way to Los Angeles County after the fall of Saigon in 1975.

"They cannot find jobs, they don't have furniture, just sit on the floor," said C. P. Cheung, a California State University, Los Angeles, professor who helped round up volunteers to lend a hand in resettling "the boat people."

A 1977 survey led to projections of an Anglo minority in the city within three years, when blacks were expected to make up 21.5 percent of the population, Hispanics 27.5 percent and Asians and Pacific Islanders 6 percent. The newcomers from Asia and the Pacific Islands had such "an appetite for hard work, long hours and frugal persistence," the *Times* reported, that they enjoyed the lowest high school dropout rate of any ethnic group in Los Angeles (an estimated 4.7 percent) and the highest percentage of persons above the age of twenty-four who had finished college (30.3 percent).

Tom Kagy Nahm, a Korean-American law student, expressed anger in a *Newsweek* essay (January 15, 1979) at the stereotype of the "quiet, industrious, submissive Oriental." Much has been written about the success story of young Asian-Americans who have become doctors and engineers, he pointed out, but in California, where 20 percent of medical students were Asian, they accounted for only about 4 percent of law-school enrollments.

"Asian children," he concluded, "have apparently been conditioned by the stereotype to feel that for them success should be achieved through quiet study in fields that do not require them to confront whites, as in the courtroom."

Robert M. Takasugi is an exception. He spent three years of his boyhood in a Japanese-American internment camp, where, he says, "I saw the total destruction of dignity in my mother and father and others around me." He completed his undergraduate work at UCLA, studied law at USC (Class of 1959) and in 1970 served as national counsel for the Japanese-Citizens League. In the spring of 1976 he was appointed to the U.S. District Court, the first Asian-American to sit on the federal bench in Southern California.

Little Tokyo, the sixty-eight-acre cultural and commercial center for Southern California's 110,000 Japanese-Americans, is home for about 700 Angelinos, many of them first-generation immigrants who live quietly in small hotel rooms above shops. Some have moved into the new Little Tokyo Towers (301 units), but others, who had counted on 1,000 new housing units at the start of the community's $100,000,000 redevelopment program a dozen years ago, have been displaced by restaurants, banks, the New Otani Hotel and the Japanese Village Plaza, with nearly fifty specialty shops.

When Nancy Yoshihara, a *Times* reporter, took a close look at the hub of the Japanese-American community in April, 1980, she found a wide variation of views among landlords and tenants, employers and and employees as to what Little Tokyo should be.

"Overall," said Bruce Iwasaki, a member of the Little Tokyo People's Rights Organization, "we want to see Little Tokyo become a thriving community, but not dependent on a tourist economy or Japanese businessmen who come to crash out and find a good time."

The number of Korean Angelinos increased dramatically during the decade, reaching a total of 58,421 in 1977. They have put their stamp on Koreatown, an area bounded by Alvarado and Crenshaw, Pico Boulevard and Third Street. K. W. Lee, editor of *Koreatown Weekly*, deplores the community's lack of political leadership, but sees hope in the younger generation ("they are wiser than we are") and in the churches ("Korean churches, just like the early black churches, play the role of an extended family. Our future leaders may emerge from our churches, like Martin Luther King").

The influx of blacks, Mexicans, Chinese, Japanese, Cubans, South Americans, Indochinese, Filipinos, Samoans, Armenians, Greeks, Serbs, Croatians and Lithuanians has enriched and enlivened the city, giving it a rich ethnic mix of neighborhoods where Angelinos with Iowa in their blood can sample exotic foreign dishes and wash them down with native wines and beers.

"Within ten blocks on Figueroa," writes Richard E. Meyer of the *Times*, "Colonel Sanders sells California kosher burritos. T. B. Chew sells Famous Chinese Herbs and a woman everyone calls Sister sells barbecue beef and pork. The Orpheum Theater, where Al Jolson played in blackface, shows Anglo movies with Spanish subtitles. Students in Glendale Unified School District speak forty-four languages, including Filipino Tagalog and Arabic. Cherif Zein, born in Egypt, reared in Morocco, speaks Spanish, French and Arabic, teaches English-as-a-second-language and has coached Glendale College to a soccer championship.

"Koreans, rich and poor, sweep the streets of Koreatown with brooms, the way they did at home. Their Americanized brethren in Arcadia drive into town on weekends to eat Korean and buy a jar of *kimchee*. The Filipino-American newspaper *Balitaan* is so culturally proud that it refuses to print the letter F because the Philippine alphabet has no F. A Buddhist temple in Chinatown has a Boy Scout troop."

* * *

"The California version of the American dream may be dying," readers of the *New York Times* learned from Lawrence Van Gelder in 1979, but a poll taken by the *Los Angeles Times* found that while nearly two-thirds (65 percent) of New Yorkers thought things were going badly in their city, more than half of the sampled Angelinos (54 percent) were satisfied with things at home. Residents of both cities agreed that New Yorkers were ruder and more self-centered. They also thought New Yorkers were more cultured.

"I feel the electricity here," Zubin Mehta said when he took over the New York Philharmonic Orchestra.

The flamboyant, forty-two-year-old "macho maestro," as *Newsweek* called the Los Angeles defector, was replaced by Carlo Maria Giulini, the reserved, sixty-five-year-old conductor of La Scala and Rome Opera, who reminded local reporters that Igor Stravinsky, Bruno Walter and Arnold Schoenberg had once lived in their midst.

"This is a young orchestra," he said, and he might have been using it as a metaphor for the world of his new neighbors when he added, "they don't know what it is to give routine performances."

It has become the journalistic fashion to dub Los Angeles "the ultimate city" or "the prototype of supercity," an idea that occurred to Bruce Bliven in 1927 when he referred to the booming metropolis as "a melting pot in which the civilization of the future may be seen bubbling darkly up in a foreshadowing brew." Now that the boulevards of the earth's major cities are all clogged with motorists crawling through the same noxious haze in search of a place to park, a current cliche paraphrases Lincoln Steffens' remark on his return from the Soviet Union in 1919: "I have seen the future, and it doesn't work."*

The Central City's new skyline towers above the universal problems of congestion, pollution, poverty and lawlessness, none of which is new to the pueblo. Main Street in 1910 was described by the *Times* as a mixture of "skyscrapers and hovels." Young hoodlums were stealing buggy whips in the 1880s and hubcaps in the 1970s. A Los Angeles banker, in 1930, unburdened himself of the thought: "Modern criminals do not seem to have any fear of the law. A mistaken leniency on the part of many judges has much to do with this."

Sheriff Peter J. Pitchess, in 1972, defied the National Rifle Association by supporting a proposal to outlaw handguns. "Our society is experiencing a catastrophic upheaval," he told a congressional subcommittee. Seven years later about half of the country's 20,000 murders a year involved handguns. Los Angeles, with a population of less than three million, reported 804 murders in 1979, seven times the number of homicides in the Greater London area, with a population of more than 7 million. POLICE PLAN TO LIST ALL SHOOTING IRONS, the *Times* reported on June 13, 1908 when the city's acting chief of police instituted "a sweeping crusade against the promiscuous sale of firearms."

In his first moments as mayor-elect in 1973 Tom Bradley promised "to start digging a rail rapid transit system within a year and a half." Seven years later Angelinos were still standing on street corners waiting for a bus. In 1887 the American Rapid Transit Company had presented a plan for an elevated electric monorail line from Pasadena to Santa Monica designed to whisk its passengers high above horse-drawn carriages at a speed of one hundred miles an hour. The cost was estimated at $1 million. When a similar suggestion was made in the mid-Fifties the tab was put at $165 million.

Air pollution is regarded as a disagreeable by-product of modern technology, with the gaseous exhalations of the internal combustion engine singled out for the heaviest share of the blame, but

---

* His actual words were, "I have been over into the future, and it works."

in 1877, before Angelinos had seen their first bicycle, much less their first horseless carriage, a City Council committee, choking on the dust swirling up from the unpaved streets of the business district, warned that air pollution in downtown Los Angeles was so bad "it does not allow invalids with lung disease to remain here."

By rights, no metropolis of such magnitude should have sprung up on the Yangna villagers' hunting grounds, but Angelinos have always managed to do the unexpected. The founding fathers grew more grain than anyone had thought possible. Their successors proceeded to raise more cattle, press more wine, ship more oranges, pump more oil, pick more flowers and build more fighter-bombers than even the most ebullient prophets had foreseen.

"Life in Los Angeles is a tonic," the *Times* chirped in 1906, when it was rounding out its twenty-fifth year. "Optimism, hopefulness, and courage are in the air. As one comes downtown in the morning one feels ready for the day's battle, like a giant refreshed with new wine."

The giant, in each generation, has kicked aside the pueblo's past to make way for its future. Street-builders in the 1880s casually destroyed the site of Fort Moore. Fifty years later the historic hill was chewed up for a continuation of Spring Street. The dirt was hauled a few blocks away to improve the approaches to the new Union Passenger Terminal and, in the process, bury old Chinatown.

"Those lots on Bunker Hill will double in value in one year," the *Star* predicted in 1874, when Prudent Beaudry carved out the city's first hillside subdivision.

As the city moved west toward the sea, men who had grown old and rich buying and selling, lending and speculating, healing and suing, abandoned Bunker Hill to fling up French chateaux and English manor houses on the recycled beanfields of Beverly Hills. The Gothic mansions of their childhood were left to a mixed lot of pensioners, prostitutes and petty criminals.

"In the tall rooms haggard landladies bicker with shifty tenants," Raymond Chandler wrote in *The High Window* (1942). "On the wide cool front porches, reaching their cracked shoes into the sun, and staring at nothing, sit the old men with faces like lost battles."

The faded nineteenth-century elegance and the unwanted twentieth-century decay have now been pushed aside to provide high-rise accommodations ("You can live above it all at the Bunker Hill Towers") within walking distance of the city's center for the performing arts, the West's financial heartland and the country's most massive congeries of government buildings this side of the Potomac.

West-end burghers who in the old days would have lived long and possibly useful lives without ever setting foot in downtown Los Angeles except to answer a jury summons are now dining at the Pavilion, the Tower or Bernard's before taking in a play or a concert at the Music Center. An earlier generation would have eaten at Good Fellow's Grotto on South Main Street before going on to the Belasco or the Hippodrome. When it closed in December 1953, Good Fellow's was the city's oldest restaurant. It was forty-eight.

"It used to be a place where people retired," Isamu Noguchi said when he came home to Los Angeles in 1980 with his design for a one-acre plaza in Little Tokyo to serve as the focal point for the Japanese-American Cultural and Community Center. The seventy-five-year-old sculptor had no intention of retiring. "I am just passing through here," he said, and described himself as "a mixture from the pre-liberation, pre-hippie era, a kind of throwback to the liberalism of the Yeats and Pound generation."

If the grandchildren of the Japanese athletes who took part in the 1932 Olympiad come to the 1984 Games in Los Angeles, they will not go home with stories of racial slurs. Instead of being turned away from public places, they will discover some of the more imposing buildings in the Central City are owned by their fellow-countrymen. Mitsubishi contributed a substantial chunk of the $110,000,000 required to build the five 35-story cylindrical towers of the Bonaventure Hotel. Another Japanese company, Mitsui Fudosan, picked up the 42-story Crocker Plaza for $79,000,000.

The dollar's shrinking value in the 1970s brought investors not only from Asia, but also from Europe, Canada and the Middle East. They gobbled up what seemed to them bargains in real estate. When a 1.5-acre parcel at Fifth and Figueroa came up for sale, all four bidders turned out to be Canadian. The action on Broadway, a downtown Mexican fiesta where shopkeepers peddle everything from bridal gowns and plastic souvenirs to bedroom suites and $390 ostrich skin shoes, is financed in part by Korean capital.

"The weather is nice and the land is cheap compared to overseas," says Fred Chan, a young investor-developer from Hong Kong by way of Berkeley and Harvard, who spends Asian and Canadian money. He helped put together the Asian Tower, a Chinatown shopping complex designed for Chinese and Vietnamese merchants. The land cost $1,000,000. In his native Hong Kong it would have brought four times as much.

"I find a city flush with enthusiastic life and filled to the brim with business," a visitor wrote the editor of the *Los Angeles News* in 1867, and a local antiquarian, preparing a paper for a later generation of Angelinos, declared in 1905: "The new Los Angeles is one of the most unique cities of modern times."

It is still flush with enthusiastic life, still filled to the brim with business, still new, still unique and still erasing yesterday's landmarks to clear space for full-scale models of tomorrow's megalopolis. In view of the odds against the pueblo at the outset (can eleven illiterate families with twenty-two children find happiness in a heathen wilderness?), there seems to be a sporting chance that the future may work.

Los Angeles Miscellany

ANGELS FLIGHT
On grand opening day, New Year's Eve, 1901, passengers got a free ride and a dollop of fruit punch. The Third and Hill Street landmark was dismantled in the spring of 1969. Its two orange-and-black cars, Olivet and Sinai, are preserved at the Heritage Museum, 1200 Olive St. Angels Flight was not the city's first cable car line. That distinction belongs to the Second Street Cable Railroad, which on October 8, 1885 made its pre-opening trial run, using a dummy as its passenger.

AREA
Under the terms of its Spanish land grant of 1781, El Pueblo's original area was four square leagues (twenty-eight square miles), but when the city hired an attorney to appear before the United States Land Commission in the 1850s to confirm its title to the pueblo lands, he applied for an area four leagues square, which would have given his client a royal legacy of sixteen square leagues (112 square miles). He settled for four. The city's physical growth was stunted until 1895 when it took off on an annexation spree which began with Highland Park. It added the sober, God-fearing community of Hollywood in 1910 and a chunk of the San Fernando Valley five years later. The city's 315-mile boundaries now encompass an area of 463.7 square miles.

AUTOMOBILES
In the early morning hours of Sunday, May 30, 1897, J. Philip Erie bundled his wife and half a dozen friends into a four-cylinder, gasoline-powered horseless carriage he and S. D. Sturgis had put together in a West Fifth Street shop at a cost of $30,000. "This innocent-looking black tally-ho has about twenty-five miles an hour concealed in its vitals," the *Times* reported next day, and went on to predict that it would "not be long before a factory is established in Los Angeles for the manufacture of motor wagons."

By 1915, with 55,217 cars distributed among its 750,000 inhabitants, Los Angeles County led the world in the per capita ownership of automobiles. It still does.

BANKS
"We have now emerged from a country town to an inland city," the *Los Angeles News* noted on January 10, 1868, when a steamer from San Francisco arrived at San Pedro with iron for the vault of the city's first bank, James A. Hayward & Co. Some months later, on September 1, Isias W. Hellman, F. P. F. Temple and William Workman opened a Main Street bank "with fire-proof iron front," which evolved into Farmers & Merchants National Bank. It merged in 1956 with Security-First National. Around the turn of the century, banking moved west from Main to Spring Street, which in an earlier day had served as the stable entrance for Main Street mansions.

BEER
Lager beer was brought down from San Francisco in 1853 and produced locally the following year. The National Prohibition Amendment took effect on January 16, 1920. It was backed up by local ordinances a year later. Legal beer began to flow again April 7, 1933.

BICYCLES
The first recorded tryout of a velocipede occurred on April 25, 1869 when a carriage-maker's apprentice took a tumble at the junction of Main and Spring Streets. By 1883 wheelmen were careening about the streets at such a clip that pedestrians called on the City Council to draft an ordinance requiring them to install bells and lights as warning devices. Nearly a century later, in 1980, freeway signs were urging fuel-conscious motorists to use "pedal power" and BIKE TO WORK. Long-range plans were afoot to link the business district with the San Fernando Valley and South Central Los Angeles by building a bikeway along the shoulders of the Los Angeles River.

BRADBURY BUILDING

In the early 1890s, having made a fortune mining in Mexico, Louis Bradbury decided to run up a monument to himself in the form of a downtown office building. Disappointed in the plans of Sumner P. Hunt, a leading Los Angeles architect, he offered the assignment to a young draftsman in Hunt's office, George Herbert Wyman, who had no formal education in architecture. He turned the job down, but one Saturday evening when he and his wife were huddled over a planchette board (a forerunner of the Ouija board), Wyman picked up a message from his dead brother: "Take Bradbury Building. It will make you famous." Eighty years after its completion, architects still make pilgrimages to Third and Broadway to enjoy its inner court bathed in sunlight and to admire its bird-cage elevators, marble paneling, Mexican floor tiles and delicate ironwork. Nothing in the heart of the pueblo is so ageless and joyful. Shortly after he finished work on the building in 1893, Wyman signed up for a correspondence course in architecture and created no more masterpieces.

CATHOLICS

Of the country's 49,812,178 Roman Catholics (1980), 2,069,682 live in the Los Angeles archdiocese, the second largest in the United States. Chicago, with 2,400,000 ranks first; Boston, with 2,010,000, third.

CEMETERIES

The pueblo's first cemetery serves as a parking lot for the county's venerable Brunswig Building, 513 North Main Street, next door to the Plaza Church. Apparently the more socially prominent remains were removed before the land was reconsecrated to the use of the automobile. An additional cemetery, marked out north of the Plaza in 1844, was reached by way of Calle de Eternidad (Eternity Street). In the 1930s it gave way to the Pasadena Freeway.

CITY HALL

An adobe house across the street from today's City Hall sufficed to accommodate both city and county government in 1853. The City Council moved to a two-story brick building at 213 West Second Street in 1884. Four years later it moved again, this time to a red sandstone-and-tile structure on Broadway between Second and Third. Municipal government came back to its old haunts on April 26, 1928 with the dedication of its new $4,800,000 skyscraper City Hall (twenty-eight stories). It had cost $20,000 less than anticipated. The final tab for the City Hall East-Mall South is expected to exceed $40,000,000, a cost override of from $3,000,000 to $5,000,000.

CONVENTION CENTER

"They've torn up so many buildings for freeways, it used to be that when you got downtown there was nowhere to go," Bob Hope commented on July 10, 1971, when the city opened its new $43,000,000 Convention Center, where 8,000 delegates with plastic name-tags can be fed at a sitdown dinner. It was here, in September, 1973, that Vice President Spiro Agnew assured the National Federation of Republican Women he would never resign. He handed in his resignation the following month, on October 10.

COUNTY COURTHOUSE

After holding court for a few months in 1850 in a ramshackle adobe, the county rented space at the Bella Union Hotel, situated at about what is now 314 North Main Street. In May, 1861, court convened on the first floor of the building known as "City Hall and Market House," near the northeast corner of the present-day City Hall. On August 8, 1891, a few months after the birth of Earl Warren (March 19) a few blocks away (457 East Turner Street), six Superior Court judges moved into a new red sandstone courthouse on the corner of Temple and Broadway. Chief Justice Warren delivered the dedicatory address on October 31, 1958, when the cornerstone was laid for the present courthouse, sealing such documents as the county's business license ordinance, a statement of bonded indebtedness and the regulations of the Air Pollution Control District.

DRUG STORE

"I will teach them how to take medicine," twenty-three-year-old John G. Downey said in 1850 when an old Los Angeles hand advised against opening a drug store in "the healthiest country in the world." With James P. McFarland as his partner, the personable young Irishman set up shop in a small adobe building on the northwest corner of Los Angeles and Commercial Streets. Three years later, having accumulated $30,000, he began buying up land, including the site of the city which now bears his name.

FIRE DEPARTMENT

In December, 1865, when San Franciscans talked of establishing a paid fire department, the *Los Angeles News* snorted: "By all means pay the firemen one or two hundred dollars per month; the taxpayers of San Francisco are rich and can afford it." A volunteer firefighting force "to consist of not more than three steam fire engine companies" was created by the Los Angeles City Council on December 8, 1871. The firemen were added to the municipal payroll on December 1, 1885. They got $100 a month.

GRIFFITH PARK

Colonel Griffith J. Griffith appeared before the City Council on December 16, 1896 with an unexpected Christmas gift of 3,015 acres, the world's largest city park. It lay outside the corporate limits until 1910. Its present area is 4,063.87 acres, which makes it larger than Beverly Hills (3,646.7 acres).

HALL OF RECORDS

The venerable landmark, built at a cost of $1,063,644, was the seat of the county government for half a century (1911-60). Like the

Old Red Courthouse on Poundcake Hill, it was originally aligned with New High Street. When the street was obliterated, the Hall of Records was left standing at an odd angle, like a mildly dotty old lady caught in the crush of civic center traffic. In 1938 and again in 1962 the Board of Supervisors looked into the possibility of relocating the 25,000-ton building, but finally gave up the idea and earmarked it for demolition to make way for an underground garage with a landscaped roof. The new Hall of Records was dedicated May 18, 1962. It cost $11,700,000 and may age with grace and dignity, but is not likely to remind anyone of an elderly aunt who has been nipping at the cooking sherry.

ICE

When Wells Fargo & Company opened an express office in Los Angeles in 1857, it was commissioned to bring the city its first shipment of commercial ice. The undertaking proved to be a financial disaster. In the spring of 1868, when a wagon operating from a Main Street depot started daily deliveries of ice brought by steamer from the Truckee River, the *Los Angeles News* hailed it as "another step forward in the progress that is to make us a great city." A few weeks later the editor watched a demonstration of an ice-making machine imported from Paris, France. "What next?" he wondered. Machine-made ice went on sale in the city April 14, 1871.

ICE CREAM

When Matilda Newmark married Maurice Kremer, April 1, 1856, the bride's father served ice cream. It was, so far as Harris Newmark could remember, the first time Angelinos had tasted it. An ice cream salon, using locally manufactured ice, opened on Spring Street in Temple Block in the early spring of 1871.

JEWS

The first Jewish services were held in Los Angeles shortly after the arrival of Joseph Newmark in 1854. The city's first synagogue, a brick building on the east side of Fort Street (Broadway), between Second and Third, was dedicated on August 8, 1873. Only Israel and New York City now have more Jews than the 472,000 who live in Los Angeles.

LIBRARY

"The absence of a place where a cultivated person may go for books of reference or standard library works has been spoken of to our injury abroad." the *Star* noted on December 5, 1872. That night some 200 Angelinos met at the Merced Theater and formed a library association. "An original letter by Lord Byron is on view at the library room," the *Star* announced the following spring. The ordinance establishing the public library passed the City Council on March 7, 1878. The central library moved to its present home, 630 West Fifth Street, in July 1926. With its sixty-two branches, it now circulates more than 12,000,000 books a year. In 1963 the Los Angeles Library Association was resuscitated to lend the librarians a friendly hand.

MOTION PICTURES

On May 10, 1909, Hobart Bosworth, a New York actor who refused to let his name be associated with the enterprise, wrote in his diary: "All Saturday and yesterday I acted as leading man before a kinetoscope, a strange but not unpleasant experience." His scene for *In the Power of the Sultan* was filmed in a Chinese laundry on the west side of Olive Street, just north of Eighth. In 1903 the Electric Theater, 262 South Main Street, became what is thought to be the first theater in the country to devote itself exclusively to the showing of moving pictures.

NEWSPAPERS

The city's first newspaper, the *Star*, made its debut May 17, 1851, and after many vicissitudes folded in the early part of 1879. The *Weekly Mirror* first appeared on February 1, 1873. Later that year, on October 2, the *Herald* began publication. It created quite a stir as the first Southern California newspaper to be printed by steam presses. The first issue of the *Times* hit the streets on December 4, 1881. The editor hoped the Republican candidates for city council would prevail in the following day's election. They didn't.

OIL

Indians used the basin's deposits of *brea* (the tar was congealed petroleum) to caulk their boats and waterproof their woven baskets. Pioneer Angelinos covered the roofs of their adobes with it to ward off the rain. In 1855 General Andres Pico sold it as a lamp oil and a medicine. The city's first oil boom, 1864-67, was shortlived, but another boom was touched off in November, 1892, when Edward L. Doheny dug a well near Second Street and Glendale Boulevard. On June 23, 1921, a geyser of crude oil shot up from the depths of a Long Beach hill where early-day Angelinos used to signal ships at sea. In the next fifty years the more than 2,400 wells of Signal Hill produced 859,000,000 barrels of oil. The two-square-mile area incorporated in 1924 and elected the state's first woman mayor, Mrs. Jessie Elwin Nelson.

OLVERA STREET

Originally Wine Street, it was renamed for one of its most distinguished residents, Agustin Olvera, the first county judge. Thanks to a posse of influential crusaders rounded up by Mrs. Christine Sterling in 1928, the filthy, decaying alley was refurbished with prison labor. "Each night," Mrs. Sterling wrote in her diary, November 21, 1929, "I pray they will arrest a bricklayer and a plumber." The Mexican *paseo*, with its string of shops, booths and eating places, was thrown open to the public on April 20, 1930. "Happiness," wrote Mrs. Sterling, "lingers here as it did in the old days."

PARKING METERS

In the late spring of 1949, newfangled hitching posts sprang up in North Hollywood along Lankershim Boulevard from Cumston to

Hartsook Streets. On Monday, June 12, police began issuing tickets for motorists who neglected to deposit five cents in the parking meters for a one-hour stay.

PERSHING SQUARE

On December 11, 1866, Mayor Cristobal Aguilar signed an ordinance setting aside five acres of the pueblo's royal land grant as "a Public Square or Plaza, for the use and benefit of the Citizens in common...." It went by various names (Public Square, City Park, Central Park, Sixth Street Park, among others) until November 18, 1918, when the city fathers, caught up in the exuberance of Armistice Day, named it Pershing Square.

PLAZA

The original Plaza was a 200-by-300-foot rectangle northwest of the present-day site. The shift occurred in 1818. "A magnificent ruin," the *Herald* declared in 1874, and in the summer of 1896 the park commissioners were restrained by the city attorney and a group of outraged antiquarians from turning the pueblo's birthplace into a public market. It is now a 44-acre State Historic Park administered by the city.

PLAZA CHURCH

Although nine miles separated the pueblo's first families from the spiritual resources of Mission San Gabriel, they waited three years before they got around to building a chapel of their own. Another twenty-three years slipped by before they laid the cornerstone of the Nueva Iglesia (New Church) in 1814. The site was flooded the following year and the church moved to higher ground, thus shifting the center of the pueblo. Its Spanish land grant was measured one league (about 2.6 miles) to each wind from the middle of the church door. By the time the church was dedicated on December 8, 1822, Spain's flag had been replaced by the eagle and serpent of the Mexican Empire.

PLAZA DE LA RAZA
For years the recreation center of the East Los Angeles barrio has been Lincoln Park, three miles from the downtown district. In 1969, when local authorities tagged the park's venerable boathouse for demolition, the Chicano community came up with a plan for a Plaza de la Raza cultural center which would include administrative offices in the boathouse, along with a Ruben Salazar Memorial Performing Arts Center, a library, museum and workshops.

POWER POLES
The first pole for the overhead lines of the Bureau of Power and Light was erected in the northeast section of the city at the corner of Pasadena Avenue and Piedmont Street, March 30, 1916. Fifty-five years later the Mayor's Council on Environmental Management, reporting on visual pollution, noted that there were "approximately 6,400 miles of overhead power lines throughout the city."

PRETZELS
"Pretzels have made their appearance in Los Angeles," the *Star* announced, June 21, 1871.

PRONUNCIATION
"There is no other city in the world whose inhabitants so miserably and shamelessly, and with so many varieties of foolishness, miscall the name of the town they live in," Charles F. Lummis wrote a friend in 1914. He was still shuddering at the memory of hearing Theodore Roosevelt refer to the city as "Loss-AN-gee-lees." Lummis advocated a pronunciation in which "Los" rhymed with "Dose," the A in Angeles was slightly broader than the A in "Arm," the G was hard and the final "es" rhymed with "Yes." He spelled it phonetically: LOCE *ANG*-ELESS.

PROTESTANTS

On a June Sunday in 1850, in a private home near the present site of City Hall, a Methodist minister named J. W. Brier conducted the first Protestant service held in Los Angeles. The first Protestant church was established in 1853 on unhallowed ground where, two years earlier, a pair of army officers had opened a saloon, El Dorado. The two-story structure, made of prefabricated lumber shipped around the Horn from Boston, was the pueblo's first wooden building. When the saloon fell on lean days, the Reverend Adam Bland bought it and converted it to a Methodist Church. It was later razed to clear space for the Merced Theater.

RADIO

"Radiating their voices over the Southwest by the marvel of the wireless and vacuum amplifier of the radiophone, Clifford Lott and Corinne Harris last night entertained with vocal selections," the *Times* reported on April 18, 1922, and began publication of a daily chart indicating "the exact time various stations will be 'on the air.'" A year and a half later, the paper noted, "the radio craze has spread around the globe faster than the influenza."

RAILROADS

The first railroad south of the Tehachapis, the Los Angeles & San Pedro, was formally opened on October 26, 1869 and gobbled up by the Southern Pacific three years later. On September 5, 1876, a golden spike driven into the SP tracks at Lang Station, near Newhall, linked Los Angeles by rail with San Francisco and the East Coast. In May 1939, when Angelinos spent three days celebrating the completion of the Union Passenger Terminal, sixty-four trains roared in and out of the city every day. On May 1, 1971, when Amtrak (National Railroad Passenger Corp.), a quasi-governmental operation, took over passenger service for the country's railroads, there were only fifty-two trains a week. But Southern Pacific, "The Octopus" which had once held California politics in its tentacles, remains the state's largest private landowner (2,000,000 acres).

SANTA ANAS

Angelinos are occasionally caressed or battered by a hot, dry wind which has been compared to the *foehn* of the northern Alps and the *hamsin* of the Middle East. Named for the cañon through which they often blow, the Santa Anas occur when air rushes down from the high inland plateaus, sweeps through mountain cañons and bursts suddenly on the lower coastal valleys. Compression heats the air as much as 5.5° for every 1,000 feet of vertical drop, at the same time expelling much of the humidity. The natives are noticeably restless during a Santa Ana. Anything can happen, Raymond Chandler once noted. "Meek little wives feel the edge of the carving knife and study their husbands' necks."

SERVICE STATIONS

Earle C. Anthony, a Los Angeles Packard dealer ("Ask the Man Who Owns One"), toured France in 1912 and, according to William A. Spalding, he "observed that every 100 kilometers or so along main highways there was a sign, 'Petrol,' and that when a car drove up to that sign a man carrying a hose stepped out and pumped as many liters of gasoline into his tank, through the hose, as were ordered . . ." That interested him, as then, in this country, it was customary for one to drive into a garage or up to the village grocery and have gasoline poured into the tank from a five-gallon can. On his return home, Anthony told H. L. Arnold what he had seen, and together they worked out an adaptation of the idea. As soon as they could arrange it, they opened, at Grand Avenue and Washington Street, what probably was the first service station in America." The claim provokes an argument in Seattle, where a Standard Oil engineer was dispensing gasoline from a 30-gallon hot water tank as early as 1907.

SMOG

When Juan Rodriguez Cabrillo spotted the brownish haze of Indian fires hanging above the hunting grounds of Southern California, he gave the name *Bahia de los Fumos* (Bay of the

Smokes) to what was either the bay of Santa Monica or San Pedro. Four centuries later, on July 27, 1943, under the front-page headline: CITY HUNTING FOR SOURCE OF "GAS ATTACK," the *Times* reported the fourth assault of a "smoke nuisance." A year later, on September 18, a new word passed into the local lexicon when the paper, using an expression common in Pittsburgh, referred to the bronze pall as "smog (smoke and fog)."

STREET LIGHTS

In the pueblo's early days, homeowners on travelled streets were required to hang a lighted lantern in front of their doors on dark nights. A proposal to light the city "by a new process called Aubin gas" was placed before the council in 1857, but not until May 5, 1866 did the city fathers grant a franchise for the erection of a gas works. The councilmen got into an argument with the gas company in 1872 and the company cut off the city's service. Los Angeles claimed to be the first city in the country to be entirely lighted by electricity when its mayor, on New Year's Eve 1882, switched on the current for the new public lighting system. Electric lights, warned gas company propagandists, would cause color blindness and ruin the ladies' complexions.

SUBURBS IN SEARCH OF A CITY

Of all the cliches about El Pueblo, none is more persistent than the designation of Los Angeles as a varying number of suburbs in search of a city. When it cropped up in the London *Daily Telegraph* in 1972, Jack Smith suggested in his *Times* column that originally it was "forty suburbs." No one, not even the incomparable Mr. Smith, knows for sure how the thing got started, but the leading authority on such matters, the late W. W. Robinson, was convinced that the phrase dated back to the 1920s when somebody linked the city's urban sprawl with the newly published English translation of Pirandello's play, *Six Characters in Search of an Author*.

TAXICABS

The West's first taxicab, loosed on the city streets on June 16, 1908, by the enterprising Mr. Anthony (see SERVICE STATIONS), proved to be an immediate success. The fare was 30 cents for the first half-mile, 10 cents for each additional quarter-mile. "There is no reason," observed the *Times*, "why a dozen cabs cannot be kept busy here." They still could.

TELEGRAPH

Los Angeles and San Francisco were linked by telegraph October 8, 1860. The first news story sent by wire advised readers of the San Francisco *Bulletin*: "The steamer *Senator* leaves San Pedro tonight with about three thousand boxes of grapes."

TELEPHONES

The Los Angeles Telephone Company, on April 15, 1882, issued its first directory (three pages), instructing users to call the central office ("Ring 'two bells' ") and then "give the telephone number and not the name of the subscriber wanted." Three months later the *Times* reported that the home of the chief of police had just been "connected with the telephone system."

THEATER

The city's first English-speaking theater opened July 4, 1848 in an addition to the home of Don Antonio Coronel. William Abbott's Merced Theater was inaugurated December 30, 1870. It shared a common wall with the Pico House, enabling hotel guests to enter and leave the red plush boxes without having to step outside. Abbott was a thin, nervous man, uxorious and ordinarily unshaven. His wife, the formidable Doña Mercedes (née Garcia), and their nine children held down the third floor, while the family breadwinner looked after the theater on the second floor and the furniture store below it. He also moonlighted in the basement as an undertaker.

TRAFFIC LIGHTS

As the city was celebrating the one hundred and fiftieth anniversary of its founding in early September 1931, motorists were getting used to the experimental three-light traffic signals on Wilshire Boulevard between Westlake Park and the west city limits. They were equipped with "a soft-toned gong to signify a change," the *Times* reported, and explained that "the top light is the red 'stop,' the center and amber 'caution' and the bottom one the green 'go.' "

TRAFFIC SIGNS

Boulevard stop signs first appeared at the city's more hazardous intersections in September, 1923, and received a warm welcome from both motorists and pedestrians.

TRANSPORTATION

The city's mass rapid transit system began in September 1873, with two horse-drawn cars which the *Star* described as "splendid and easy-riding omnibuses." The following summer, on July 2, R. M. Widney's Spring and Sixth Street line went into operation. Its owner used it to commute to the office from his country home on Hill Street between Fourth and Fifth. The last horse-drawn streetcar vanished from the city in 1897. On Independence Day, 1902, a crowd of 30,000 turned out to watch a big red car of Henry E. Huntington's Pacific Electric Railway complete the interurban line's first scheduled run to Long Beach. Trolley buffs climbed aboard for the final run on April 8, 1961. Buses were brought in to supplement the local service of the Los Angeles Railway's historic yellow cars on October 10, 1923, but by then more than one-third of city's commuters were driving to work in their own automobiles. The last streetcar retired from service on March 31, 1963. It reached the car barn ten minutes late.

TRIFORIUM

The theme tower of the Civic Center Mall, billed as the world's first kinetic color-music sculpture, has three 60-foot pylons housing a computer capable of synchronizing the music of Mozart and Gershwin. It has been called "The Trifoolery," "The Glass Harmonica," "The Psychedelic Nickelodeon" and "The Million-Dollar Jukebox" (its actual cost was around $925,000). "It will outlive the critics," says its creator, Joseph L. Young, who deplores the low esteem in which artists are held these days. "Once we advised kings, and now the postman isn't even courteous."

UNION PASSENGER TERMINAL

The city's three major railroads—Southern Pacific, Santa Fe and Union Pacific—should build a common terminal, a planning study recommended in 1911, and six years later the City Council put up $20,000 to look into the proposal. The union station should be built near the Plaza, Angelinos decided at the polls in 1926, but railroad lawyers managed to keep the project tied up in litigation until 1933, when their clients finally agreed to drop the fight. A crowd estimated at half a million showed up to inspect the $11,000,000 terminal when its massive doors opened on Wednesday, May 3, 1939. The first train pulled in at 6 o'clock the following Sunday morning.

WATER

The founding fathers lost no time in digging a *zanja madre* (mother ditch) to provide water for their fields and for domestic use. The *zanja* system lasted until 1903. Meanwhile, in 1868, the city fathers granted a thirty-year monopoly on the distribution of water to a few influential neighbors who had formed a private company. In 1897, as the contract was about to expire, the water company was serving 100,000 Angelinos, but, under the terms of its contract, the City Council was powerless to order a rate reduction below the figures originally set for a town of 15,000. The city acquired the water system for $2,000,000 on February 2, 1902. The Department of Water and Power is now the country's largest municipal utility operation.

WATTS TOWERS

"I had in mind to do something big, and I did," Simon Rodia explained after he'd spent thirty-three years building his three towers (99, 97 and 55 feet high) at 1765 East 107th Street of seashells, tiles, broken bottles and salvaged lengths of iron and steel. When his work was done in 1954, he moved to Martinez, where he died July 17, 1965 without ever having revisited what had come to be regarded as a triumph of twentieth century folk art. In October 1961, two years after bureaucratic vandals in the city's Department of Building and Safety had tried in vain to have the towers torn down (the artist had neglected to take out a building permit), Rodia met with some students at Berkeley, "Do the best you can," he said, when asked what advice he had for young people, "but the way it's going we have so many lawyers we may some day have to get a permit to go to bed."

WEATHER

The *Star's* daily temperature readings were taken from the bookstore thermometer at 13 Spring Street before a U.S. Signal Corps sergeant opened the city's first weather bureau on July 1, 1877. The city's record high, 110°, was established on September 1, 1955; the record low, 27.9°, on January 4, 1949.

YANGNA

The five hundred or so brush huts of Yangna, one of many aboriginal villages in the vicinity, disappeared within fifty years of the pueblo's founding. In 1836 the city's decimated Indian population was crowded into a ghetto near what is now the southeast corner of Commercial and Alameda Streets, an area often mistakenly identified as the original site of Yangna. Its actual location cannot be pinpointed, but was probably within bow and arrow range of present-day City Hall.

SOURCES

Abbreviations:

    LAT: Los Angeles Times
    NYT: New York Times
    HSSC: Historical Society of Southern California
    UCLA-SC: University of California, Los Angeles, Special Collections, University Research Library

Chapter 1

p. 10   "Some Americans despise Los Angeles..." *Washington Post*, 7 June 1974.

p. 10   "In Los Angeles, you never feel weird..." El Monte High School student, quoted by Jack Smith, LAT, 12 April 1973.

p. 11   "What changes do you expect..." At a breakfast, 16 January 1980, Century Plaza Hotel.

p. 11   "We gave them a little tobacco..." Herbert Eugene Bolton, *Fray Juan Crespi: Missionary Explorer on the Pacific Coast* (Berkeley: University of California Press, 1927), p. 147.

p. 12   "We have our surf and sand..." Jack Smith, LAT, 16 May 1977.

p. 15   "The Indians were sadly afraid..." Robert F. Heizer, ed., *Hugo Reid's Letters of 1852.* (Los Angeles: Southwest Museum, 1968), p. 69.

p. 17   "healthy, robust..." HSSC, *Annual Publications* (1931): 192.

p. 18   "probably the most extensive..." Charles Dwight Willard, *The Herald's History of Los Angeles City* (Los Angeles: Kingsley-Barnes & Neuner, 1901), p. 75.

p. 21   "den of thieves." Sir George Simpson, *Narrative of a Journey Round the World, during the Years 1841 and 1842* (London: Henry Colburn, 1847), I, 402.

p. 22   "the catacombs of ancient Rome..." Leonardo Cota, Quoted by W. W. Robinson, *What They Say About the Angels* (Pasadena: Val-Trefs Press, 1942), p. 12.

p. 22   "In the hands of..." Richard Henry Dana, *Two Years Before the Mast*, ed. John Haskell Kemble (Los Angeles: Ward Ritchie Press, 1964), p. 172.

p. 23   "They are cultivating farms..." Joseph Warren Revere, *A Tour of Duty in California* (New York: C. S. Francis, 1849), p. 25.

p. 23   "a person could travel..." Hubert Howe Bancroft, *California Pastoral* (San Francisco: History Co., 1888), p. 273.

p. 24   "As the savages faded..." Ibid., p. 293.

p. 24   "When Indians died..." Bernice Eastman Johnston, *California's Gabrielino Indians* (Los Angeles: Southwest Museum, 1964), p. 189.

Chapter 2

p. 25 "Time, flood..." "The Plan of Old Los Angeles." HSSC, *Annual Publications* (1895), III: Part 2,42.

p. 27 "We commenced..." *Glances at California, 1847-1853* (San Marino: The Huntington Library, 1942), p. 20.

p. 28 "An antiquated, dilapidated..." Robinson, *What They Say*, p. 16.

p. 28 "But one solitary brick..." Thompson & West's *History of Los Angeles County*, with introduction by W. W. Robinson (Berkeley: Howell-North, 1959), p. 91.

p. 29 "Los Angeles, prosperous..." Robert F. Lucid, ed., *The Journal of Richard Henry Dana, Jr.* (Cambridge: Harvard University Press, 1968), III, 848.

p. 30 "The brute upshot..." W. W. Robinson, *Land in California*. (Berkeley and Los Angeles: University of California Press, 1948), p. 12.

p. 30 "The effect on the individual..." W. W. Robinson, *The Indians of Los Angeles* (Los Angeles: Glen Dawson, 1952), p. 3.

p. 36 "The November term grand jury..." Paul M. De Falla, "Lantern in the Western Sky." HSSC *Quarterly* (June 1960): 173.

p. 44 "Colonel Otis and I..." Turbese Lummis Fiske and Keith Lummis, *Charles F. Lummis: The Man and His West* (Norman: University of Oklahoma Press, 1975), p. 33.

p. 44 "Landowners were repeatedly..." Glenn S. Dumke, *The Boom of the Eighties in Southern California* (San Marino: The Huntington Library, 1966), p. 45.

p. 46 "tortured with pain..." Walter Lindley and J. P. Widney, *California of the South* (New York: D. Appleton, 1888), pp. 74-75.

p. 48 "no great importance..." Karl Baedeker, *The United States With an Excursion into Mexico, A Handbook for Travellers*, 1893 (reprinted by Da Capo Press, New York, 1971), p. 445.

p. 49 "prove very troublesome..." Charles Fletcher Lummis, *Landmarks Club Scrapbook* (Los Angeles: Southwest Museum) Report to City Council filed Feb. 11, 1897.

Chapter 3

p. 51 "The northern half of California..." H. L. Mencken, *Saturday Night*, (8 January 1927), 3.

p. 52 "HOMEWARD BOUND..." LAT, 4 December 1906.

p. 59 "Los Angeles is a busy centre..." Karl Baedeker, *United States* (Leipzig: 1909), p. 534.

p. 63 "When an oil belt..." William A. Spalding, *History and Reminiscences of Los Angeles* (Los Angeles: J. R. Finnell & Sons, 1931), I, 332.

p. 66 "soothed and satisfied..." LAT, 3 January 1900. Cf. Ralph Hancock, *Fabulous Boulevard* (New York: Funk & Wagnalls, 1949), pp. 85-112.

p. 67 "Whereas, the morals..." Filed 30 August 1897 [City Council Report] Vol. 50, p. 41.

p. 68 "I was raised..." John D. Weaver, "1909". *Westways* (February 1979), 20 ff.

p. 69 "just once in order to teach..." Marco Newmark, *Jottings in Southern California History* (Los Angeles: Ward Ritchie Press, 1955), p. 60.

Chapter 4

p. 72 "Our studio consisted of..." Mary Pickford, *Sunshine and Shadow* (Garden City, N.Y.: Doubleday, 1955), p. 128.

p. 72 "We have tried..." LAT, 10 October 1909.

p. 74 "I stood across the street..." W. W. Robinson, *Bombs and Bribery* (Los Angeles: Dawson's Book Shop, 1969), p. 1.

p. 75 "Since 1901..." Grace Stimson, *Rise of the Labor Movement in Los Angeles*, (Berkeley: University of California Press, 1955), p. 368.

p. 76 "You hear talk..." Ibid., p. 368.

p. 76 "The greatest enemies..." Ibid., p. 370.

p. 77 "They had it on us..." LAT, 6 December 1911.

p. 77 "It was my intention..." Ibid.

p. 78 "For socialism..." John Caughey, *California* (Englewood Cliffs, N.J.: Prentice-Hall, 1953), p. 478.

p. 78 "one of the famous Spanish dinners..." LAT, 14 January 1912.

p. 80 "The house darkened..." William de Mille, *Hollywood Saga* (New York: E. P. Dutton, 1939), p. 57.

p. 81 "memories of the milk can..." W. H. Wright, "Los Angeles—The Chemically Pure." *Smart Set* (March 1913). Reprinted in Burton Rascoe and Groff Conklin eds., *The Bachelor's Companion* (New York: Grayson, 1944), pp. 90-102.

p. 82 "a world-center..." Harris Newmark, *Sixty Years in Southern California* (Los Angeles: Zeitlin & Ver Brugge, 1970), p. 651.

p. 83 "With a gangrened heart..." David Halberstam, *The Powers That Be* (New York: Alfred A. Knopf, 1979), p. 103.

p. 84 "Harry, I want you to go..." LAT, 31 July 1917. Cf. Robert Gottlieb and Irene Wolt, *Thinking Big* (New York: G. P. Putnam's Sons, 1977), p. 117.

Chapter 5

p. 88 "more people died..." LAT, 28 December 1919.

p. 88 "No mere virtuous city..." LAT, 4 August 1918.

p. 89 "The map of Los Angeles..." Series of six articles, LAT, beginning 12 November 1923.

p. 92 "six solid years of hell..." Albert W. Atwood, *Saturday Evening Post* (12 May 1923), 10.

p. 92 "Day after day..." Ibid.

p. 96 "My daughter, Myrabel..." H. L. Mencken, *Americana, 1926* (New York: Alfred A. Knopf, 1926), p, 17.

p. 98 as Will Robinson recalled... "The Southern California Real Estate Boom of Twenties." HSSC *Quarterly Publication* (March 1942), pp. 25-30.

p. 102   "Aimee Semple McPherson was born knowing..." Lately Thomas (Robert V. Steele), *The Vanishing Evangelist* (London: Heinemann, 1960), p. 98.

p. 103   "I am going to give..." James Thorpe, "The Founder and His Library," *The Founding of the Henry E. Huntington Library and Art Gallery* (San Marino: The Huntington Library, 1969), p. 303.

p. 104   "Great book collectors..." LAT, 24 May 1927.

p. 104   "The world is periodically scourged..." John D. Weaver, "Ralph Bunche: The Early Years," *Westways* (May 1975), 18.

p. 106   "I envy the dead." Remi A. Nadeau, *The Water Seekers* (Garden City, N.Y.: Doubleday, 1950), p. 121. Cf. LAT. 12 March 1978, San Fernando Valley ed., and Charles F. Outland, *Man-Made Disaster: The Story of St. Francis Dam* (Glendale, Calif.: The Arthur H. Clark Co., 1977).

p. 107   "in recognition of the growing needs..." Advertisement, *Los Angeles Examiner*, 25 September 1929.

p. 107   "an expression of modern art..." From an unpublished press release, quoted by David Gebhard in *The Richfield Building 1928-1968* (Atlantic Richfield Co., n.d.).

Chapter 6

p. 109   "The situation is not at all alarming..." Duncan Aikman, "California Sunshine," *The Nation* (22 April 1931), 448.

p. 110   "official confession..." Ibid.

p. 112   "God has rolled away..." LAT, 14 September 1931.

p. 114   "matchless climate..." Jackson Graves, *California Memories* (Los Angeles: Times-Mirror Press, 1930), p. 2.

p. 117   "a dark, crowded section..."NYT, 3 August 1930.

p. 117-8   "the dullest and most..." Robert Benchley, *Yale Review* (September 1931), 103.

p. 118   "slum of Africans..." Aldous Huxley, *After Many a Summer Dies the Swan* (New York: Harper & Bros., 1939), p. 5.

p. 118   "Let the people establish the precedents..." LAT, 29 November 1932.

p. 118   "It hit hard..." Matt Weinstock, *My L.A.* (New York: A. A. Wyn, 1947), pp. 233-234.

p. 119   "This idea of ..." NYT, 14 July 1932.

p. 119   "Thousands thronged the city..." NYT, 9 October 1932.

p. 119   "leader of the National Socialist Party..." LAT, 13 December 1931.

p. 120   "The old order..." LAT, 24 March 1933.

p. 120   "The factories were idle..." *The Autobiography of Upton Sinclair* (New York: Harcourt, Brace & World, 1962), p. 269.

p. 120   "The fundamentalist..." Leon Harris, *Upton Sinclair: American Rebel* (New York: Crowell, 1975), p. 301.

p. 121   "How would California..." Ibid., p. 319.

221

p. 122	"He dicated some notes..." John D. Weaver, *Warren: The Man, The Court, The Era* (Boston: Little, Brown, 1967), pp. 43-44.	
p. 122	"The greatest single nuisance..." Ibid, pp. 76-83.	
p. 122-3	"One of the princely wits..." LAT, 23 July 1935.	
p. 125	"Imagine driving your car..." LAT, 16 February 1938.	
p. 127	"most modern terminal..." LAT, 2 January 1940.	
p. 127	"It is a dream of empire..." LAT, 20 November 1939	

Chapter 7

p. 129	"A neighbor told us..." *Daily News*, 9 December 1941.
p. 130	"I knew the situation..." LAT, 8 December 1941.
p. 132	"The gunfire..." *Newsweek*, "Those Weren't Japs," (12 November 1945), 67.
p. 132	"the subsequent testimony..." LAT, 25 February 1962. Cf. also LAT, 25 February 1979.
p. 133	"They are being well fed..." LAT, 26 December 1941.
p. 134	"We're charged with..." Frank J. Taylor, "The People Nobody Wants," 9 May 1942, p. 66, quoted in Weaver, *Warren*, p. 108.
p. 134	"Race does not lie..." Carey McWilliams, *North From Mexico* (New York: Greenwood Press, 1968), p. 234.
p. 134	"The Caucasian..." Ibid.
p. 135	"Being strangers..." Ibid., p. 242.
p. 138	"dumps, lumberyard incinerators..." *Newsweek*, (23 December 1946), 27.
p. 139	"The good Lord..." *Time* (4 July 1949), 13.
p. 143	If one day...Material on 6 February 1947 from various contemporary sources, including LAT, *Daily News* and *Congressional Record*.

Chapter 8

p. 149	"What happened to the Okies..." *US. News & World Report* (16 September 1955), 65.
p. 149	Jeanne Parry material from Jack Smith, LAT, 14 November 1979.
p. 149	"It was the day of ducktails..." LAT, 24 January 1979.
p. 149	"all a girl needed..." Jack Smith, LAT, 22 October 1972.
p. 150	"It started with..." "Happy Birthday to a Dream, Disneyland 25," an advertising supplement, LAT, 20 January 1980, p. 7.
p. 150	"Light is one thing..." LAT, 2 October 1952.
p. 151	"You've got to place McCarthy..." *Playboy* (June 1956), 54.
p. 151	"except in certain remote areas..." *The Reporter* (9 January 1958), 35.
p. 151	"That's easy to say..." *Time* (15 August 1960), 43.
p. 154	"I would like to see a National League team..." A 1954 statement quoted in LAT, 14 April 1958. Cf. also Penelope McMillan article, LAT, 4 June 1978.
p. 155	"They even applauded..." James Gow, the playwright, to a friend, circa 1959.

p. 156 "While Brooklyn..." *The New Yorker* (17 October 1959), 33.
p. 157 "In its traditional..." LAT, 8 March 1949.
p. 158 "Welcome to Los Angeles..." Norris Poulson, "Who Would Have Ever Dreamed?" Unpublished autobiographical typescript (1966), UCLA-SC.
p. 159 "We do not agree..." Ibid.

Chapter 9

p. 162 "things were just as bad..." Theodore Sorenson, *Kennedy* (New York: Harper & Row, 1965), p. 294.
p. 163 "contains all the diverse elements..." Jules Witcover, *85 Days: The Last Campaign of Robert Kennedy* (New York: G. P. Putnam's Sons, 1969), p. 233.
p. 164 "I like 'em..." LAT, 24 August 1964.
p. 165 "The test for a dirty book..." LAT, 7 April 1966.
p. 165 "In fact, it may be..." *The Reporter*, (18 January 1962), 40.
p. 165 "Oh my goodness..." LAT, 1 July 1964.
p. 165 "All of my fears..." Weaver, *Warren*, p. 252.
p. 166 "This is a historic day..." LAT, 4 November 1960.
p. 166 "symbol of the steady upsurge..." *Time* (18 December 1964), 46.
p. 166 "Perhaps no one..." Halberstram, *Powers*, pp. 268-269.
p. 167 "Early in the campaign..." Ibid., p. 347.
p. 167 "We cannot build enough..." LAT, 15 May 1964.
p. 168 "I have not seen an application..." LAT, 17 May 1973.
p. 168 "walk-in mental health..." Caskie Stinnett, *Speaking of Holiday*, (March 1963).
p. 168 "come in like a swarm..." LAT, 29 July 1961.
p. 169 "Here I am..." letter, 24 July 1941, Aldous Huxley Collection (No. 2009), UCLA-SC.
p. 169 "its size, rapid growth..." George W. Robbins and L. Dering Tilton eds., *Los Angeles: Preface to a Master Plan* (Los Angeles: Pacific Southwest Academy, 1941), p. 5.
p. 171 "I'd be out of sorts..." LAT, 13 August 1965.
p. 171 "The majority of people..." LAT, 23 March 1975.
p. 172 "If we don't win..." Gladwin Hill, *Dancing Bear: An Inside Look at California Politics* (New York: World, 1968), p. 238.
p. 172 "It's where the action is..." *Newsweek*, "The Teenagers" (21 March 1966), 75.
p. 173 "Every day people are straying..." John D. Weaver, "The Fault, Dear Bruce, Is Not in Our Stars." *Holiday* (November 1968), 72.
p. 173 "I like good old Anglo-Saxon words..." Ibid.
p. 174 "I haven't let loose..." LAT, 12 April 1969.
p. 175 "...it shows what can be done." *The New Republic*, "Fallen Angels" (7 June 1969), 7.

p. 175   "We have tried to prove..." *The Nation*, (16 June 1961), 749.

Chapter 10

p. 177   The morning after... LAT, 31 May 1973

p. 178   "you can get a job..." LAT, 3 June 1973.

p. 178   "Watts had a phenomenally high..." "Bradley Not Yorty," *The New Republic* (9 June 1973), 8.

p. 178   "I'd rather wait..." LAT, 31 May 1973.

p. 179   "where you are now..." LAT, 30 June 1974.

p. 180   "that he sought out homosexuals..." Richard Reeves, "Boom", *The New Yorker* (24 December 1979), 74.

p. 181   "Well, we're a *little* insane." LAT, 10 September 1978.

p. 181   "the housing crisis..." LAT, 18 November 1979.

p. 182   "I've committed adultery..." *Playboy* (November 1976), 86.

p. 182   "Women and men now talk..." LAT, 9 May 1980.

p. 182   "We have come through..." LAT, 5 April 1972.

p. 183   "we lost the power..." LAT, 10 October 1972.

p. 183   "These illegal aliens..." LAT, 19 August 1979.

p. 184   "We're all in the same boat..." Ibid.

p. 185   "Here in Los Angeles..." *Radicalism Exposed*, speeches delivered at the 14th annual convention of California peace officers, Pasadena, Oct. 4-6, 1934, published by the Peace Officers of the State of California, n.d.

p. 186   "overcrowded, tense and tawdry..." *Negro Digest* (October 1947), 9.

p. 186   "This is the most segregated city..." LAT, 4 July 1962.

p. 186   "for the citizens..." Charlotta A. Bass, *Forty years; memoirs from the pages of a newspaper* (Los Angeles, 1960), p. 14.

p. 187   "Segregated education..." LAT, 21 January 1980.

p. 187   "Do you believe..." LAT, 29 December 1978. Interview with Robert Scheer.

p. 188   "You know it..." Ruben Salazar quoted in *Los Angeles Daily Journal*, 9 August 1972.

p. 189   "Unlike the Negroes..." LAT, 27 February 1963.

p. 189   "I sometimes feel..." LAT, 30 August 1971.

p. 192   "We're fighting with the blacks..." LAT, 30 July 1978.

p. 192   "We would certainly..." LAT, 13 April 1980.

p. 193   "I saw the total destruction..." LAT, 7 May 1976.

p. 194   "they are wiser..." LAT, 13 April 1980.

p. 194   "Within ten blocks..." Ibid.

p. 195   "I feel the electricity..." *Newsweek* (18 December 1978), 73.

p. 195   "a melting pot..." *The New Republic* (13 July 1927), 197.

p. 196   "Modern criminals..." Jackson A. Graves, *California Memories* (Los Angeles: Times-Mirror Press, 1930), p. 283.

p. 196   "to start digging..." LAT, 30 May 1973.
p. 198   "In the tall rooms..." Raymond Chandler, *The High Window* (New York: Alfred A. Knopf, 1942), p. 65.
p. 198   "It used to be..." LAT, 31 March 1980.
p. 199   "The weather is nice..." LAT, 3 September 1979.

LOS ANGELES MISCELLANY
BANKS
p. 201   "with fire-proof iron front." Robert Glass Cleland and Frank B. Putnam, *Isias W. Hellman and the Farmers & Merchants Bank* (San Marino: The Huntington Library, 1965), p. 16.

BRADBURY BUILDING
p. 202   "Take Bradbury Building..." *A Vast Hall Full of Light*, (history prepared by the Los Angeles Cultural Heritage Board, n.d.)

DRUG STORE
p. 204   "I will teach them..." Hubert Howe Bancroft, *Chronicles of the Builders of the Commonwealth* (San Francisco: History Co., 1892), II, 124.

MOTION PICTURES
p. 206   "All Saturday..." LAT, 9 May 1949.

OLVERA STREET
p. 207   "Each night I pray..." Christine Sterling, *Olvera Street: Its History and Restoration* (Los Angeles: Old Mission Printing Shop, 1933), p. 18.

PRONUNCIATION
p. 209   "There is no other city..." Letter to J. M. Guinn, in Lummis Papers, Southwest Museum, published LAT, 22 January 1914.

SANTA ANAS
p. 211   "Meek little wives..." "Red Wind," reprinted in *The Midnight Raymond Chandler* (Boston: Houghton Mifflin, 1976), p. 7.

SERVICE STATIONS
p. 211   "observed that every 100 kilometers..." Spalding, *History and Reminiscences*, p. 372.

TRIFORIUM
p. 214-5   "It will outlive..." Barbara Isenberg. "A Merging of the Human Senses," *California Business* (3 October 1946), 11.

WATTS TOWERS
p. 216   "I had in mind..." *The Watts Towers* (booklet published by the Committee for Simon Rodia's Towers in Watts, n.d.)

Index

Abbott, William, 213
Adamic, Louis, 87, 94
Adobes, 10, 19, 22, 28, 29, 33, 82, 203, 204, 207
  disappearance of, 33-34, 48
Agnew, Spiro, 203
Agriculture, 15, 17, 20, 89, 125, 139, 169, 197
Aguilar, Cristobal, 208
Ahmanson Theater, 166
Air Conditioning, 82, 107, 171
Air Raids, 130-132, 168
  shelters, 149, 150
Alexander, George, 68, 76, 77
Alhambra, 17, 114
Aliens, Illegal, 183-184
Allender, F. W., 186
All In The Family (television), 182, 183
Alta California, 13, 15, 20, 183
Ambassador Hotel, 158, 161, 163-164
American Federation of Labor, 76, 78
American Rapid Transit Company, 196
Amtrak, 210
Angels Flight, 200
Angels, Los Angeles, 154
Angelus Temple, 100, 102, 112, 117, 121
Annexation, 53, 55, 200
  and water, 54, 79, 89
Anthony, Earle C., 211, 213
Aqueducts, 52, 53-54, 106, 113, 127
Arbuckle, Roscoe (Fatty), 96-97
Arcadia, 194
Arcadia Block, 28
Architecture, 10, 100, 202
  height-limitations, 107

Arcaro, Eddie, 144
Area, 11, 25, 46, 54, 55, 89, 200
Argüello, José, 19
Arnold, H. L., 211
Asians, 117, 192-195, 198-199
Atchison, Topeka & Santa Fe Railroad, 44, 215
Atlantic Richfield Plaza, 10
Atomic Energy, 115, 127
Audubon, John W., 28
Automobile, 63, 67, 68, 69, 86, 94, 202, 211
  dependency on, 93, 142, 168
  first, 60, 200
Automobile Club of Southern California, 125
Aviation, 69, 111-112, 115, 143, 149
Avila Adobe, 81
Avila, Encarnación, 24
Aylesworth, M. H., 124

Baja California, 13
Baedeker's Guidebooks, 48, 59
Baker Block, 97
Bancroft, Hubert Howe, 23, 24
Bandini, Juan, 21
Banducci, Enrico, 151
Banking, 52, 63, 85, 107, 193, 199
  history of, 201
Banning, Phineas, 34-35
Bara, Theda, 83
Baseball, 29, 47, 151
  Dodgers deal, 154-156
Beaches, 47, 112, 115
Beatles, 164
Beaudry, Prudent, 55, 58, 197

Beer, 40, 194, 201
Bel-Air, 11, 164
Bel-Air Hotel, 144
Belasco Theater, 198
Bell, Eric Temple, 115
Bell, Horace, 137
Bella Union Hotel, 62, 137, 203
Benchley, Robert, 97, 117-118
Benny, Jack, 133
Bergholz, Richard, 167
Bergman, G. Merle, 12
Berkeley, 120, 127, 178, 216
Beverly Hills, 19, 117, 133, 143, 184, 197
  area, 204
Beverly Hills Hotel, 97, 163-164
Beverly Hilton Hotel, 167
Bicentennial, 183
Bicycles, 64, 201
Biggs, Peter, 184
Billboards, 66, 115,123
Biltmore Theater, 144
Biograph Film Company, 71-73, 78
Birth of a Nation, The (film), 81
Bitzer, G. W. (Billy), 71
Blacks, 36, 117, 118, 192
  and Chicanos, 183-184, 189
  and Communism, 150-151
  heritage, 18, 111,184
  population, 118 (1900-1930), 185 (1910-1920), 186 (1930-1960), 192 (1980)
  in Watts, 170-171, 178
Bland, Adam, 210
Bliss, Leslie, 104
Bliven, Bruce, 98, 165, 195
"Boat People," 182, 192
Boggs, Francis, 72
Bonaventure Hotel, 199
Boom of the Eighties in Southern

California, The, 44-45
Boosterism, 42, 46, 53, 55, 92, 110, 138, 205
  second thoughts about, 170
Boston, 22, 28, 48, 139, 202, 210
Bloomer Girls, 47
Bosworth, Hobart, 206
Bowron, Fletcher, 125, 139, 142, 148
Boyce, H. H., 43
Boyle Heights, 17, 47, 189
Bradbury Building, 202
Bradbury, John, 98
Bradbury, Louis, 202
Bradley, Tom, 10 (1980), 174-175 (1969), 177-179, 196 (1973)
  on integration, 187
Brandeis, Louis, 83
Brea (tar), 15, 22, 60-61, 207
  fossils in, 69
Brentwood, 11, 164
Bricks, 10, 28, 33, 48, 64
Brier, J. W., 210
Brookins, H. H., 171
Brooklyn, 154-156
Broughton, Diane, 163-164
Brown, Edmund G., 167, 169-170
Brown, Edmund G., Jr., 149
Bruce, Lenny, 173-174
Bullock's-Wilshire, 107
Bunche, Ralph, 104-105
Bunker Hill, 166, 197, 198
Burbank, 20, 59, 111, 143
Burns, William J., 137
Byrd, Richard E., 144
Byron, George Noel Gordon, Lord, 206

Cabrillo, Juan Rodríguez, 13, 211
California, 13, 195

legislature, 51, 143, 165-166, 180, 189
and Mexico, 20, 22-24
north-south rivalry, 51-52
population, 169-170, 188, 193
and Spain, 13, 35
California Club, 52, 166
California Tomorrow, 168-169
Carlisle, Kitty, 125
Carnation Company, 139
Carr, Harry, 97-98
Carrillo, José Antonio, 10, 21, 29
Carrillo, Leo, 110
Carter, Jimmy, 182
Case, Fred, 180-181
Catholics, 51, 102, 144
number of, 202
Caughey, John, 78
Cayton, Horace R., 186
Cemeteries, 27, 202
Central City, 10, 94, 114, 137, 196
foreign investments in, 198-199
Century Plaza Hotel, 172
Chamber of Commerce, 92, 157
Chan, Fred, 199
Chandler, Alberta, 166
Chandler, Dorothy Buffum (Mrs. Norman), 166
Chandler, Harry, 54, 84, 120
Chandler, Marian Otis, 84
Chandler, Otis, 166
Chandler, Philip, 166
Chandler, Raymond, 198, 211
Chapman, Joseph, 20
Chavez Ravine, 154-156, 165
Cheung, C. P., 192
Chicanos, 117, 118, 119, 192, 209
alienation of, 188
and blacks, 183-184, 189
discrimination against, 134-137
in politics, 188-189

Childs, Ozro W., 99
China, 167
Chinatown, 36, 192, 195, 197, 199
Chinese, 36, 41, 206
and law, 37-38
massacre of (1871), 36-40, 137
and other minorities, 117, 192
population, 36 1870), 192 (1970s)
Chinese Chamber of Commerce, 192
Chu, Irene, 192
Churchill, Winston, 106
City Council, 30, 49, 66-67, 74, 93, 100, 197, 201, 204, 206, 215,
and Dodgers, 154-155
land, 27, 55-58, 112
mayor, 107, 189
minority members, 178, 188-189
oil, 60
City Hall, 46, 55, 67, 142
first, 20
1928 building, 36, 100, 203, 210, 216
Civic Center, 69, 115, 144, 167, 198, 205, 214
Climate, 30, 72, 143, 199, 211
and health, 19, 46, 114
record temperatures, 216
Cline, Herman, 102-103
Coliseum, 118-119, 155
Colorado River, 106, 113, 127
Columbia Broadcasting System, 156-157, 182
Comecrabit, Victoria Bartoloméa (Mrs. Hugo Reid), 15
Commerce, 20, 29, 112
Communism, 109, 149, 150-151, 165
Khrushchev visit, 157-159
and sex, 185-186
Compton, 59, 142
Connell, Kathleen, 181
Conrad, Paul, 166

Convention Center, 203
Coolidge, Calvin, 118
Cornero, Tony (Antonia Stralla) 123-124
Coronel, Antonio, 213
Courthouse, County, 46, 203, 205
Crespi, Juan, 11
Crime, 28, 30, 88, 97, 134, 170, 188
  "of the century," 73-78
  past and present, 196
Crosby, Bing, 125

Dana, Richard Henry, 9, 22-23, 29
Darrow, Clarence, 76-77, 94
Davis, Anne, 184
Davis, Ed, 171
Davis, Grace Montanez, 188
Davis, James E., 185-186
De Forest, Lee, 114
DeMille, Cecil B., 79-80, 157
DeMille, William, 80
Democratic Convention (1960), 162
Depression (1930s), 109-110, 114, 118, 135, 149, 179
Descriptions,
  1781-1849: 18-19, 21-23, 24, 27-30, 33
  1850-1899: 10, 41-43, 44, 47-49, 97-98, 140
  1900-1909: 55, 59, 67, 199
  1910-1919: 81-82, 196
  1920s: 92, 94, 97, 98, 107, 140
  1930s: 116-118, 119
  1940s: 139-140, 142
  1950s: 147-148
  1960s: 167-169, 170
  1970s: 10, 12, 93, 195-196
  1980: 11, 193-194
Developers, 33, 34, 49, 93
DeWitt, John L., 132
Díaz, José, 135

Discrimination, 104, 119, 134-135
Disneyland, 150, 158
Disney, Walt, 150
Dodgers, Los Angeles, 154-156
Doheny, Edward L., 60, 207
Dominguez Field, 69
Dominguez, Juan José, 20
"Donation Lots," 58
Don Lee, 68, 124
Doolittle, James H., 111
Dorothy Chandler Pavilion, 166
Douglas, Helen Gahagan, 145
Downey, John G., 204
Dress, 12, 83, 114-115, 139
Drinking, 20, 21, 22, 29, 30, 40, 117, 118, 134, 162
Drive-ins, 9, 82, 168
Drugs, 149, 172-173, 179
Drug Stores, 204
Drunkard, The (melodrama), 144
Dumke, Glenn S., 44
Dunbar Hotel, 118
Dykstra, Clarence, 169

Earthquakes, 11, 12, 15, 63, 74, 120, 143, 145
East Los Angeles, 46-47, 189, 209
Eaton, Fred, 53
Ebbets Field, 154
Eccentricities, 81, 98, 116, 138, 165
Edendale, 72, 78-79
Egly, Paul, 187
Einstein, Albert, 115
Eisenhower, Dwight D., 151, 154, 158, 166
Electric Theater, 206
Electricity, 48, 82, 212
Elysian Park, 11, 58
England, 21, 23, 25, 85
  and Hollywood films, 78
Erie, J. Philip, 200

Ethnic Mix, 111, 117, 118, 192-195

Fads, 148, 149, 165, 181-182
Fairbanks, Douglas, 97, 98, 110, 114
Farmer's Market, 116
Farmers & Merchants National
   Bank, 201
Farnum, Dustin, 80
Federal Bureau of Investigation,
   130, 133
Filipinos, 118, 194-195
Finney, Charles Grandison, 173
Fire Department, 58, 131, 140
   history of, 204
Fisher, Thomas, 20, 184
Fitzgerald, F. Scott, 97
Fitzherbert, Maria Anne, 27
Flags, 18, 20, 86, 208
Ford, Henry, 115
Foreigners, 20, 21
Forest Lawn, 9, 82, 117, 138, 148
Founding, 110-111
   ceremonies, 18, 111
   families, 17-19, 111, 183, 184, 199
Fox Studio, 97, 106
France, 23, 205
Franklin, Bert, 77
Freedom Riders, 174
Free Harbor League, 53
Freeways, 9, 83, 93, 125, 143, 147,
   154, 201, 202, 203
   first, 142
   in 1960s, 167-168
Frémont, John C., 24
Friday Morning Club, 83

Gabor, Eva, 156
Gagarin, Yuri, 162
Galland, Robert, 163-164
Gambling, 12, 21, 22, 29, 68

ships, 123-124
Gann, Paul, 179-180
Garden of Allah, 97
Gardner, Ava, 133
Gas, 28, 55, 63, 64, 75, 212
Gee, Robert, 192
George I, 25
Germans, 130, 133
Germany, 85, 119-120
Giants, San Francisco, 155
Giulini, Carlo Maria, 195
Glendale, 20, 78, 194
Glenn, John, 162-163, 164
Glyn, Elinor, 67
Goldwater, Barry, 166
Gompers, Samuel, 76
Good Government Organization, 68
Governors Conference (1966), 172
Grand Opera House, 46, 186
Grauman's Chinese Theater, 116
Graves, Jackson A., 114
Green, Wendell, 184
Griffith, David Wark, 71-73
Griffith, Griffith J., 204
Griffiith Park, 118, 204
Growth, 81, 92
   and environment, 47, 142, 168,
      169, 170, 178
   open shop, 113
   transportation, 59, 142-143
   water, 53, 54, 60, 89, 113
Guinn, J. M., 25

Hahn, Kenneth 154-155, 189
Halberstam, David, 166, 167
Hall, Bryant, 115
Hall of Records, 204-205
Hancock, Henry, 112
Hancock Park, 112n
Harbor, 34, 35, 88
   fight for, 52-53

in 1940s, 130
Harper, Arthur C., 68
Harriman, Job, 77, 78
Harris, Corinne, 210
Harris, Leon, 121
Harris, Lillian, 69, 121
Hart, William S., 97
Hartman, Robert, 154
Hayward & Co., James A., 201
Hazard's Pavilion, 46
Health, 46, 64-65, 144, 204
   smallpox, 17, 33
Hearst, Patricia, 182
Hearst, William Randolph, 120
Hellman, Isias W., 201
Highland Park, 200
Hill, Gladwin, 172
Hills, 33, 86, 138
   development of, 55, 68, 99, 117, 197
Hitler, Adolf, 119-120
Hollywood, 11, 59, 68, 84, 86, 93, 116 135, 174, 180
   annexation of, 200
   and motion pictures, 79-80, 117, 150, 157
   and television, 157
   in 1930s, 116-118
Hollywood Bowl, 94
Hollywood Canteen, 138
Hollywoodland Sign, 98
Holmes, Blanca, 162
Holt, Jack, 97
Homicides, 29, 30, 196
Homosexuals, 180, 182
Hoover Dam, 113
Hoover, Herbert, 84, 114
Hope, Bob, 133, 158, 203
Hopper, Hedda, 162
Horses, 15, 20, 22, 28, 29, 34
   and automobiles, 60, 86
Horsley, David, 79

House Un-American Affairs Committee, 150
Housing, 110-111, 149, 158, 170, 171, 185, 186, 188, 189
   in 1880s, 44-45
   in 1947, 145
   in 1970s, 180-181, 183-184
Hungry i, The, 151
Hunt, Sumner P., 202
Huntington, Collis P., 52
Huntington, Henry Edwards,
   and library, 103-104
   and rail rapid transit, 54, 58-59, 159, 214
Hutton, David L., 112
Hutton, William Rich, 27
Huxley, Aldous, 118, 169

Ice, 205
Ice Cream, 205
Ikkanda, Tom, 133
Immigration and Refugee Policy, Select Commission on, 184
Incinerators, 149
Indians, 11-13, 62, 83, 207
   decline of, 24, 30, 33, 216
   and settlers, 17-18
   and Spaniards, 11, 15, 17-18, 24, 30
   at work, 22, 30
Industry, 85, 89, 113, 125, 127, 169
   motion picture, 78, 94, 97, 117, 139, 157
   oil, 60, 140
   in 1940s, 139-140, 142
Inge, Dean William P., 114
Iowa, 9, 68, 194
Israel, 182, 206
Italians, 130, 133
Iwasaki, Bruce, 194

Jacobs, Andrew, Jr., 174
Jahnsen, Oscar, 123, 124
Japanese, 117, 118
  discrimination against, 119, 198
  in World War II, 130, 133-134, 193
Jarvis, Howard, 179-180
Jeans, Sir James, 115
Jessup, Roger, 137
Jews, 205-206
John Birch Society, 166
Johnson, Hiram, 83
Johnson, Lyndon B., 165, 172, 179
Johnson, Owen, 115
Jolson, Al, 194
Julian, C. C., 124-125

Kennedy, John F., 162, 163, 176, 179
Kennedy, Minnie, 100, 112
Kennedy, Robert F., 161, 163-164
  children, 163-164
Kenny, Robert W., 122
Kent State Shooting, 179
Kerby, Phil, 180
Kerouac, Jack, 150
Keyes, Asa, 102, 103, 125
Khrushchev, Nikita, 157-159
Khrushchev, Nina Petrova, 158
King, Martin Luther, Jr., 194
Koreatown, 194
Korean War, 150
Kremer, Maurice, 205
Kroeber, A. L., 30

Labor, 36, 51, 113, 144, 149
  and *The Times*, 43, 73-78
La Marr, Barbara, 97
Land, 140, 210
  and City Council, 27, 55, 58, 112
  grants, 19, 33

pueblo's royal grant, 25, 55, 58,
  200, 208
speculation, 54, 55, 58, 89, 98,
  181, 197
values, 27, 99, 199
Landmarks, 10, 197, 199, 200, 202,
  204
Lang Station, 35, 210
Las Vegas, 144, 168
Lasky Feature Film Company,
  Jesse L. 80
Lawrence, Ernest O., 127
Lear, Norman, 182
Lee, K. W., 194
Lelia Bird, 20
Levy, Al, 87
Libraries, 46, 140
  Central Library, 67, 94, 100, 206
  Huntington, 103-104
Library Association, Los Angeles,
  206
Lighting, 28, 40, 46, 58, 66
  history, 212
Lincoln, Abraham, 29, 185
Lincoln Park, 209
Lindbergh, Charles A., 103
Lindley, Walter, 46
Lindsay, Gilbert, 189
Lippmann, Walter, 120
Little Rock, Arkansas, 151
Little Tokyo, 130, 133, 193, 194,
  198
Lodge, Sir Oliver, 114
Long Beach, 20, 59, 121, 123, 214
Los Angeles High School, 68
Los Angeles Homes Company, 54
Los Angeles & Independence
  Railroad, 35
Los Angeles & San Pedro Railway,
  34, 35
Los Angeles Theater, 41

Lott, Clifford, 210
Ludwick, Ginger Timmons, 149
Lummis, Charles Fletcher, 43-44, 209
Lynn, Kenneth S., 182

MacGregor, Helen, 122
Malibu, 138
Manzanar, 134
Maps, 25-27, 89
Marina del Rey, 27
Mark Taper Forum, 166
Martin, Albert C., 183
Martinez, Richard, 189
Marvin, Lee, 182
Mason, Biddy, 184-185
Mason, Chaytor, 182
Maude (television), 178, 182
Mayer, Louis B., 120, 121
McCarthy, Charlie, 125
McCarthy, Eugene, 163, 174
McCarthy, Joseph, 149, 150-151
McFarland, James P., 204
McManigal, Ortie, 76
McNamara, James, 76-78
McNamara, John J., 76-78
McPherson, Aimee Semple (Mrs. David Hutton), 117, 120, 121
  disappearance, 100-103
  marriage, 111
McWilliams, Carey, 135-136, 140
Mehta, Zubin, 195
Mencken, H. L., 51, 88
Merced Theater, 206, 210, 213
Merchants' and Manufacturers' Association, 75
Metro-Goldwyn-Mayer Studio, 106, 121
Metropolitan Water District, 113, 114, 127
Mexico, 13, 23, 85
  independence of, 20
Meyer, Richard E., 194
Micheltorena, 49

Midwestern Influence, 66, 68, 81, 116-117, 148-149
Millay, Edna St. Vincent, 104
Miller, Loren, 110
Millikan, R. A., 115
Missions, 15, 17, 18, 30
Mississippi, 118, 186-187
Mitsubishi, 198-199
Mitsui Fudosan, 199
Monterey Bay, 15
"Monkey Trial," 94-95
Monroe, Marilyn, 150
Monterey, 20, 21
Moore, Tom, 86
Morals, 40, 66-67, 88, 96-97
Moss, Larry E., 143
Motion Picture, 12, 94, 114, 121
  colony, 78, 97, 110, 117, 151
  early days, 66, 71-73, 78-81, 206
  industry, 78, 94, 97, 117, 139, 157
  sound, 106-107, 116, 117
Motion Picture Patents Company, 72
Mount Washington, 68
Mulholland, William, 53-54, 105-106
Museum of History, Science and Art (now Museum of Natural History), 68, 140
Music Center, 166, 198

Nadeau, Remi, 48
Nahm, Tom Kagy, 193
Nakauchi, Kenji, 130
National Broadcasting Company, 124
National Rifle Association, 196
Nazimova, 97
Nelson, Jessie Elwin, 207
Nevada, 168
Neve, Felipe de, 18
New Englanders, 11, 21, 22-23
Newmark, Harris, 82, 205

Newmark, Joseph, 205
Newmark, Matilda, 205
New Otani Hotel, 193
New York
  and California, 169-170
  and Los Angeles, 148-148, 195, 206
New York Motion Picture Co., 71-72
Newspapers, 43, 110, 123, 194, 195
  black, 110-111, 175
  history, 206-207
Nieto, Manuel Perez, 20
Nixon, Richard, 166-167
Noguchi, Isamu, 198

Oil, 60-64, 115, 117
  1890s boom, 60, 140, 207
Okies, 149
Olney, Warren, III, 123, 124
Olson, Culbert, 122
Olvera, Agustin, 207
Olympic Games, 118-119, 198
O'Malley, Walter, 154-156, 165
Ord, Edward Otho Cresap, 25
Ormiston, Kenneth G., 102
Orpheum Theater, 194
Otis, Harrison Gray, 42-44, 52, 54, 144, 170
  death, 84
  and *Times* bombing (1910), 73-78
Owens, Henry, 185
Owens, Robert C., 185
Owens Valley, 53-54, 79, 89, 105, 113
  and Japanese internment, 134

Pacific Electric Railway Company, 58-59, 142, 159, 164, 214
Palms, 55
Panama Canal, 53, 54, 85

Paramount Studio, 99
Parker, William H., 171
Parking, 93, 115, 139, 147, 168, 195
  for horses, 47-48
  meters, 207-208
Parks, 134, 140, 171, 204, 208
  need for, 58, 93, .12
  oil drilling in, 60
Parry, Jeanne, 149
Parsons, Louella, 156
Parsons, Thomas, 72
Pasadena, 48, 196
  link to Los Angeles, 59, 142, 202
  Tournament of Roses, 64, 125
Pastier, John, 92-93
Pearl Harbor, 129-130, 133, 140
Pedestrians, 28, 93
Pershing Square (City Park, Central Park), 41, 85, 98, 118
  history, 208
Phillips, Cora, 36
Pickford, Mary, 71-73, 79, 80, 98
  "Pickfair", 97
Pico, Andres, 207
Pico House, 10, 40, 213
Pico, Pío, 23
Pioneer Oil Company, 62
Pioneers, 11, 82, 110
Pirandello, Luigi, 212
Pitchess, Peter J., 196
Planning, 89, 115, 139, 140-143, 169
Playboy, 150, 189
Plaza, 10, 17, 18, 19, 20, 22, 29, 40, 107, 117, 118, 127, 184, 215
  church, 21, 25, 27, 33, 202, 208
  history, 208
  land values, 28, 34
  shift away from, 46, 48, 97-98, 135, 208
Plaza de la Raza, 209

Police, 58, 66, 83, 88, 102, 123, 140, 196
   and blacks, 171, 178, 185-186
   and Chicanos, 134-137, 189
   and Chinese, 36-37
Politics, 21, 23, 149, 163, 167, 210
   and minorities, 36
   EPIC campaign, 120-122
   reapportionment, 165-166
Population,
   1836: 11, 21
   1880: 42, 47
   1900: 47, 53, 59
   1910: 59
   1920: 112
   1930: 113
   1956: 154
   1960: 165, 170
   1980: 192
Porciúncula, 11, 15, 17, 111
Pornography, 117, 144, 165
Porter, John C., 107, 109, 110
Portolá Expedition, 13, 15, 20, 22
Post, Wiley, 125
Poulson, Norris, 148
   and Dodger deal, 154-156
   Khrushchev visit, 158-159
Power, 66, 94, 113
   poles, 115, 209
Predictions, 12, 42, 47, 59, 68, 73,
   82, 93, 94, 157
   1938, as seen in 1913, 82-83
   1981, as seen in 1931, 114-116
Pretzels, 209
Prohibition, 87-89, 109, 115, 201
Pronunciation, 209
Prostitution, 20, 21, 29, 30, 41, 68, 117
Protestants, 28, 51, 66, 102, 117, 149,
   history, 210

Quintero, Luis, 19

Racism, 134-137
Radio, 111, 123, 165, 210
   and television, 124, 157
   in World War II, 131, 133
Rafferty, Max, 165
Railroads, 34, 48, 127
   depots, 34, 35, 36
   history, 210
   rate war, 44
Rancho La Brea, 68
Rancho Rodeo de las Aguas, 19
Rancho San Pedro, 20
Reagan, Ronald, 149, 172
Real Estate, 25, 28, 33, 34, 55, 63,
   68, 82, 89, 94, 117, 199
   rise in value, 34, 47, 99, 180-181,
   185, 197
Reapportionment, 165-166
Recall Process, 68, 125
Red Cross, 85
Redondo Beach, 59
Reeves, Richard, 180-181
Reibscheid, Sydney, 188
Reid, Hugo, 15, 22
Religion, 94, 173
   Indians', 13
Restaurants, 40, 81, 148, 192, 193, 198
Rexall Drug Company, 139
Rice, George, 21
Richfield Building, 10, 107
Roads, 35, 55, 64, 67, 83, 143
Robbins, George W., 169
Robbins, Harold, 67
Robinson, W. W., 30, 74, 98, 212
Rocha, José Antonio, 20
Rodia, Simon, 216
Rogers, Will, 125
Rolph, James, Jr. (Sunny Jim), 110, 118
Romney, George, 172
Rooney, Mickey, 133
Roosevelt, Franklin D., 114, 120,

122, 133, 145
Roosevelt, Theodore, 209
Rosas, Basilio, 18, 19
Rosas, José Carlos, 18
Roybal, Edward, 189
Ruiz, Eduardo, 188
Ruth, Babe, 144
Ryan, Joe, 102-103

Sabin, Albert, 150
Sacramento, 51, 143, 180
Sahl, Mort, 151
St. Francis Dam, 105-106
St. Vincent's College, 41-42, 81
Salazar, Ruben, 188, 189, 209
Salinger, J. D., 150
Salk, Jonas, 150
San Diego, 13, 53
San Fernando Mission Land
    Company, 54
San Fernando Valley, 54, 55, 62, 105
    annexation, 83, 200
San Francisco, 34, 35, 96, 109,
    145, 151, 201
    and Los Angeles, 40, 51-53, 67,
        74, 88-89, 92, 113, 139, 155, 166,
        204, 210, 213
San Gabriel, 18, 43
San Gabriel Mission, 15, 17, 18
Sanitation, 33, 41, 47, 58, 67, 82,
    139, 140, 149-150
San Joaquin Valley, 35
San Jose, 18
San Pedro, 11, 22, 35, 52-53, 59, 68,
    85, 105, 123, 186, 210, 212, 213
Santa Anas, 211
Santa Monica, 35, 40, 47, 53, 59, 81,
    115, 123, 124, 133, 181, 196, 212
Schenck, Joseph W., 99
Schoenberg, Arnold, 195
Schools, 40, 58, 94, 139, 140, 170, 188

ethnic mix in, 186-187, 188, 194
    first, 28
    desegregation, 51, 186-187
Schwartner, Michael, 150
Second Street Cable Railroad, 200
Security-First National Bank, 201
Segregation,
    in Little Rock, 151
    in Los Angeles, 184-185, 186-187
Selig Polyscope Company, 71, 73, 78
Selig, William, 72
Sennett, Mack, 71, 98-99
Service Stations, 93, 211
Shaw, Frank, 125
"Shoestring Strip," 53
Shuler, Robert, 102, 117
Sierra Club, 47, 143
Signal Hill, 207
Simpson, Sir George, 21-22, 23
Sinatra, Frank, 158
Sinclair, Upton, 83
    EPIC campaign, 120-122, 165
Sinova, José, 19
Sleepy Lagoon, The, 135
Smith, Jack, 149, 212
Smog, 83, 114, 159, 211-212
    in 1877: 197
    in 1940s: 138, 140, 142, 143,
        144, 147
    in 1960s: 168, 169, 170
Smylie, Robert, 172
Socialism, 66, 68, 77, 78, 120
Solar Heating (1910), 73
Sonora Town, 29, 33
Southern Pacific, 35, 44, 52-53,
    63, 85, 210, 215
Soviet Union, 196
    Khrushchev visit, 157-179
    space race, 154, 158, 161, 162-163
Space Exploration, 127, 154, 158,
    161, 162-163

Spalding, William Andrew, 63, 211
Spaniards, 11, 13-17, 18, 20
  and Indians, 11, 15, 17, 24, 30
Sputnik, 154
Stanton, Frank, 157
Stanwyck, Barbara, 133
Stearns, Abel, 21, 28
Stearns, Arcadia Bandini, 21, 28
Steffens, Lincoln, 195
Sterling, Christine, 107, 207
Stewart, James, 133
Stimson, Grace, 75
Stimson, T. D., 98
Stinnett, Caskie, 168
Stock Exchange, Los Angeles, 107
Stockton, Robert F., 24
Stout, William B., 115
Stravinsky, Igor, 195
Streets, 22, 47, 49
  Alameda, 34, 36, 216
  Aliso, 17
  Alpine (Virgins), 27
  Arcadia, 21, 28
  Broadway (Fort, Eternity, Buena
    Vista), 10, 11, 27, 28, 41, 46, 48,
    55, 67, 68, 74, 86, 93, 97, 107,
    125, 199, 202, 203, 206
  Central Avenue, 118, 137, 186
  Commercial, 34, 204, 216
  Figueroa (Grasshopper), 27, 60,
    82, 98, 99, 167, 194, 199
  First, 48, 60, 74, 125, 166
  Fourth, 28, 48, 135
  Frémont Place, 98
  Grand (Charity), 27, 72, 211
  Hill, 27, 28, 86, 185, 200
  Laurel Canyon, 68, 97
  Los Angeles, 28, 29, 41, 204
  Main, 21, 27, 36, 41, 44, 48, 60, 62,
    82, 97, 99, 136, 184, 196, 201,
    202, 203, 205

Micheltorena, 49
Mission Road, 17
Mulholland, 94, 106
"Nigger Alley," 29-30, 36, 37
Olvera (Wine), 107, 137, 207
Second, 28, 48, 60, 203, 206, 207
Sixth, 10, 41, 82, 99, 107, 214
Spring, 10, 27, 28, 44, 48, 67, 86,
  87, 99, 107, 125, 166, 185, 197,
  201, 205, 214, 216
Sunset, 72, 79, 97, 167
Temple, 21, 44, 60, 203
Third, 135, 194, 200, 202, 206
Wilshire, 15, 99, 107, 214
Sturgis, S. D., 200
"Suburbs in Search of a City,"
  156, 212
Sunday, Billy, 121, 173
Sunset Strip, 148, 172
Supervisors, Board of, 166, 188-189, 205
Swimming Pools, 134, 138, 185
Symbionese Liberation Army, 182

Takasugi, Robert M., 193
Talmadge, Norma, 99
Taxation, 33, 55, 67 (in 1909), 121,
  155, 165
  Proposition 13 (Jarvis-Gann), 179-180
Taylor, Robert, 133
Teale, Stephen, P., 165
Tehachapis, 34, 51, 74, 210
Telegraph Linkup, 213
Telephones, 139, 213
Television, 115, 149, 151, 154, 156-157,
  162, 165, 179
  early days, 124, 125
Temple Block, 100, 205
Temple, F. P. F., 201
Temple, John, 21, 48
Thalberg, Irving, 121

Theaters, 46, 213
Theatrical Stage Employees,
    International Alliance of, 84
Thompson, Robert, 36
Tilton, L. Deming, 169
Times, Los Angeles, 46, 52, 114,
    125, 145, 148, 156
  beginnings, 42-43, 207
  bombing, 73-78
  changes (1960s), 166-167
  and open shop, 43, 73-74, 113
Tong, Chee Long, 36
Tourists, 40, 48, 59, 78, 97, 98,
    104, 110, 117, 184, 194
Traffic, 9, 67, 93, 125, 139, 140,
    147, 167-168, 170
  lights, 214
  signs, 214
Transportation, 34, 140, 142-143,
    148, 171
  buses, 115, 116, 142, 214
  cable cars, 46, 200
  carriages and carts, 28
  elevated (1887), 196
  horse-drawn, 41, 46, 58, 98, 214
  horseless carriages, 47, 60, 197, 200
  mule teams, 41, 60
  rail rapid transit, 58-59, 60, 103,
    142, 148, 159, 164, 168, 179,
    196, 214
  taxicabs, 116, 136, 213
  trucks, 68, 85
  underground, 94, 116
Triforium, 214-215
Trinity Methodist Church, 102, 117
Triola, Michelle, 182
Truman, Margaret, 144-145
Twentieth Century Fox Studio,
    125, 158, 169, 179
Twentieth Street Elementary
    School, 179

Two Years Before the Mast, 22

Unemployment, 89-90, 110, 118,
    127, 171, 184, 185, 189
Union Passenger Terminal, 67, 127,
    158, 197
  history, 210, 215
United Nations, 105, 165, 167
Universal Studio, 79
University of California, Los Angeles,
    104, 177, 178, 180, 193
University of Southern California,
    37, 74, 151, 193
Unruh, Jesse, 169
U Thant, 105

Vallee, Rudy, 111
Van Norman, Harvey, 105
Van Nuys, 48, 83
Venice, 59, 136, 149, 162, 186
Verdugo, José María, 20
Vess, Christine, 150
Veterans, 19, 138, 139
Vietnam, 179
Vineyards, 11, 22, 27, 33, 40, 99
Vizcaíno, Sebastián, 13

Wagner, Rob, 93
Wald, Richard C., 181
Walter, Bruno, 195
Warren, Earl, 122-124, 143, 151,
    165, 203
Washington, George, 20
Washington, Leon H., 175
Water, 30-31, 40-41, 52, 55, 165
  and growth, 53, 54, 60, 89, 113
  history, 215
Water and Power, Department of,

105, 215
Watts, 11, 178
   riot (1965), 170-171, 189
Watts Towers, 216
Waugh, Evelyn, 144
Waxman, Al, 137
Wayne, John, 150
Weeks, Paul, 170
Weinstock, Matt, 118, 129-130, 143
Wells Fargo & Co., 205
Welsh, Anne, 149
Weltner, Charles L., 168
Westchester, 140
West, Mae, 144
Westlake Park, 214
Westwood, 99
Wheeler, Fred, 68
White, Stephen M., 53
Whitley Heights, 97
Whitsett, W. P., 127
Widney, J. P., 46
Widney, Robert M., 37, 214
Wilcox, H. H., 79
Wilde, Oscar, 96
Will, George F., 10
Wilmington, 34, 53
Wilshire Country Club, 99
Wilshire, H. Gaylord, 66
Wilson, Charles E., 144
Wilson, Woodrow, 83
Windsor Square, 99
Wisecarver, Sonny, 144
Women, 85, 96, 182
   first California mayor, 207
   and the vote, 69, 77, 81
Women's Christian Temperance
   Union, 87
Workman, William, 201
World War I, 83-86
World War II, 129-134, 139
Wright, Willard Huntington (S. S. Van
   Dine), 81-82, 88
Wrigley Field, 154, 155
Wyman, George Herbert, 202

Yabit, 18
Yamasaki, Minoru, 172
Yangna, 11, 15, 18, 197, 216
Yanquis, 10, 21, 23-24, 33, 49
Yorty, Sam, 159, 174-175, 177-178, 189
Yoshihara, Nancy, 193-194
Young, Clara Kimball, 93
Young, Joseph L., 215
Youth, 172-175, 179, 194

Zamorano Club, 130
Zanuck, Darryl, 125
Zein, Cherif, 194
Zeitlin, Jacob, 169
Zeman, Ray, 167
Zoot Suit Riots, 134-137

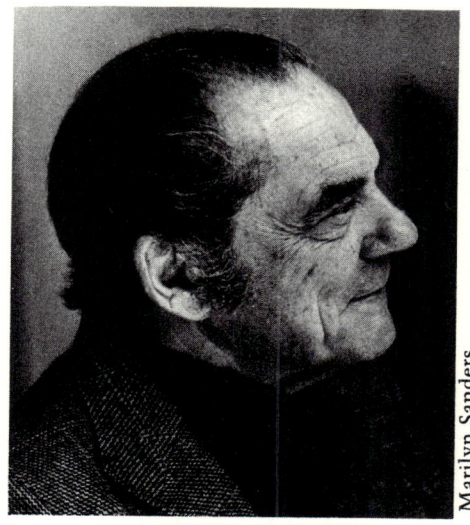

Marilyn Sanders

JOHN D. WEAVER has been an Angelino since 1940 when he and his wife Harriett "crossed the plains in a covered Chevrolet to homestead in the Hollywood hills." He is West Coast editor of *Travel & Leisure Magazine* and author of nine books and an impressive body of short stories and articles in nearly every leading publication in America. The West has become his turf and he is equally at home in a Napa Valley winecellar and the historians' table at the Huntington Library. He writes with charm, wit, and diligent research.

Weaver's witty, gracefully written book on Los Angeles combines the narrative skill of his novels and short stories with the same meticulous research that distinguished his biography of Chief Justice Earl Warren and *The Brownsville Raid*, which led to the exoneration of 167 black soldiers summarily dismissed without honor in 1906. He is also the author of the Los Angeles entry in the current edition of the *Encyclopaedia Britannica*, which Clifton Fadiman has characterized as "honest, lively, amusing and dotted with illuminating quotations from surprising sources."